PRAISE FOR *Looking for My Country*

"An unassuming, nicely qualified valentine to [MacNeil's] adopted country, a book that feels Canadian in tone and like a New Yorker's in spirit. Which makes perhaps the best argument for one of MacNeil's points—that there are, after all, many ways to be American."   —*Newsday*

"[A] conversational and appealing memoir."
                                    —*The Washington Post Book World*

"Gracefully written and pleasing in its insights and bemusements, MacNeil's memoir is a cut above the pack."   —*Booklist*

"MacNeil affirms America's better nature as a great engine of democracy and prosperity, the cockpit of social evolution, the largest home of tolerance."   —*Kirkus Reviews*

"A thoughtful and intelligent examination by a nationally famous import who found his place in a land of immigrants."
                                             —*Publishers Weekly*

"Like a latter-day de Tocqueville, MacNeil gets us—at once guileless and ambitious, generous and suspicious, absolutely inscrutable and ever open. This beautiful memoir is a thoughtful book from a man who sees America so clearly. And the country that emerges— MacNeil's country now—seems familiar, true, mine. This book is a jewel."   —Ken Burns, documentary filmmaker

"I have long known MacNeil to be a thoughtful reporter and a good writer. It is the passion here that makes the difference. This is the psychological journey of a somewhat cool Canadian who comes over time to be deeply affected by the human reality of America in ways he had not anticipated. It is very moving being on the journey with him."　　　　　　　　　　—Peter Jennings, *ABC News*

"How nice for this country that Robert MacNeil, after many, many years, became an American citizen. And, how lucky for us that he decided, in this charming, thoughtful, very nuanced book, to tell us why he did it, what is special about America, and what pulled him to becoming one of us."　　　　　　　　　—David Halberstam

"A deft, entertaining memoir, and an engagingly honest exploration of how a man comes to understand something about himself and his larger loyalties."　　　　　　　　　—Alice Munro

LOOKING FOR MY COUNTRY

LOOKING FOR MY COUNTRY

Finding Myself in America

· ROBERT MACNEIL ·

A HARVEST BOOK · HARCOURT, INC.

Orlando   Austin   New York   San Diego   Toronto   London

Requests for permission to make copies of any part of the work should
be mailed to the following address: Permissions Department, Harcourt, Inc.,
6277 Sea Harbor Drive, Orlando, Florida 32887-6777.

www.HarcourtBooks.com

First published by Nan A. Talese, an imprint of Doubleday,
a division of Random House, Inc.

Library of Congress Cataloging-in-Publication Data
MacNeil, Robert, 1931–
Looking for my country: finding myself in America/
Robert MacNeil.—1st Harvest ed.
p. cm.—(A Harvest book)
ISBN 0-15-602910-3
1. MacNeil, Robert, 1931–
2. Journalists—United States—Biography.
I. Title. II. Series.
PN4874.M18 A3 2004
070.92—dc22
[B] 2003067578

Text set in Minion
Designed by Elizabeth Rendfleisch

Printed in the United States of America
First Harvest edition 2004

A C E G I K J H F D B

For Hugh and Alison, Mike and Misia

ACKNOWLEDGMENTS

I continue to benefit immeasurably from the encouragement, insight, and good taste of my editor, Nan Talese, and the creative support of my agent, Bill Adler.

For this book, I am grateful to Annette Miller and Alice Davenport for checking the facts, dates, and names that eluded my memory.

Some incidents in this book appeared in different form, in my memoir *The Right Place at the Right Time*, which is no longer in print.

· CONTENTS ·

LOOKING FOR
MY COUNTRY

The events in our lives happen in a sequence in time but in their significance to ourselves they find their own order . . . the continuous thread of revelation.

— *Eudora Welty*

1

THE LETTER TO FDR

*I*n the winter of 1942, a couple of months after Pearl Harbor, I wrote to President Roosevelt.

I was eleven, living in Halifax, Nova Scotia. It was the third year of war for Canada, and our strategic port was a vital assembly point for convoys crossing the Atlantic to keep Britain's war effort alive. My father, a lieutenant-commander in the Royal Canadian Naval Reserve, commanded one of the corvettes protecting those merchant ships from Hitler's submarine wolf packs.

Even a boy my age could feel the high adrenaline of wartime Halifax. Men in the uniforms of many countries filled our streets; there were blackouts and air-raid drills, collections for scrap paper and metal, and the excitements of my dad's brief times ashore. Chocolate was scarce, my mother fretted over ration books for food and clothes; they built an antiaircraft gun tower beside my school, and we played war games in Point Pleasant Park. I could catch glimpses of the harbor from many places and watch gray warships of different navies slipping by—destroyers and corvettes, sometimes cruisers, even full battleships—inspiring awe and pride. Occasionally I could visit one and be taken over every inch by sailors fresh from the real war at sea.

For the rest, life was filled with school, helping with a baby brother born the day after Pearl Harbor, sledding, skating, snow forts and snowball fights, radio programs like *The Green Hornet*, movies like *They Died with Their Boots On*, comic books, real books, and my stamp collection.

My friend Harold Stevens and I were stamp collectors, but with limited pocket money we almost never bought stamps. We hoped to be given them.

We must have read about FDR's collection because it suddenly occurred to us to approach him, and I wrote something like this:

> *Dear President Roosevelt,*
> *We have heard that you have a very big stamp collection and people send you stamps from all over the world. But you must be very busy with the war right now and may not have time to play with your collection, or use all the stamps people send you. We were wondering whether you had any extra stamps you didn't want. If so we would be very happy to have them.*
> *Yours sincerely,*

How two painfully well-mannered boys found the effrontery to concoct this brazen missive, I don't know. But I stuck on the red four-cent stamp of King George VI in his wartime uniform, addressed it to the White House, Washington, D.C., U.S.A., and forgot about it.

We did not write to our king, who we knew had a stamp collection at least as fabulous as the president's. The king seemed utterly unapproachable and FDR did not.

Six weeks or more later, a letter arrived from the American consul in Halifax. Indeed, he wrote, President Roosevelt was too busy with the war to reply personally, but if we cared to come down to the consulate, he was sure they could find us some stamps. We went and were overwhelmed. They gave us a shoe box with hundreds of stamps, including exotic specimens from the Malay Straits Settlement, which had been overrun by the Japanese.

It was my first experience of American generosity. Thinking about it now, it is tempting to try to reconstruct the actions our childish letter set in motion. It would have come to a Washington still new to the turmoil of war. Compared to its size today, the White House staff was tiny and informal. But among the thousands of letters pouring in, someone had read ours, on a generous impulse had sent it to the State Department, itself a fraction of the vast bureaucracy of American diplomacy today. Someone at State decided to be nice to these kids in Halifax and sent it on to the consul, and that gentleman had to ask around his office to discover they had stamps to give us.

All this while the American government was being wrenched through the first months of global responsibility; adolescent growth spurts that were to transform the executive branch forever, from the size and modesty befitting a nation trying to mind its own business to the behemoth with the habit of minding everybody's.

I have a fantasy that on that day Eleanor Roosevelt might have been trailing through the White House mail room dispensing sympathy and patriotic encouragement to overworked volunteers, when someone showed her my childish handwriting and the Canadian stamp. "How sweet!" she exclaims. Her first impulse is to take it to Franklin, who after all has zillions more stamps than he'll ever know, but he's busy just now with Winston Churchill, who is smelling up the White House with his cigars. . . .

Or, for all I know, the letter might have been intercepted by the busybody Royal Mail in Canada and given directly to the consul in Halifax. It doesn't matter. Americans reacted with extraordinary generosity and I never forgot it.

In fact, I remembered it particularly after the attacks of September 11, 2001, listening to President Bush at a news conference:

> I'm amazed that there's such misunderstanding of what our country is about, that people would hate us. I am like most Americans, I just can't believe. Because I know how good we are.

I know how good we are. The phrase buzzed in my head as though many phone lines were ringing at once.

I know how good America is. To me personally, America and Americans have been good in measures too large to calculate. As for American goodness to its own people and to the world generally, I could probably calibrate its extent and limits objectively, and how differently goodness might be defined, historically and now. So I have a pretty confident idea of how good America is. And I know that to many, perhaps most Americans, the logic in the phrase *I know how good we are* is unassailable, admitting no irony. But I also know how such a statement might be heard by others, even by friends and allies.

I knew how it would fall on ears as sympathetic as those of America's closest friends and neighbors, the Canadians. The least paranoid would smile indulgently, but some would enjoy thinking, Typical . . . ingenuous, naive, too boastful.

In other words, the phrase would send a little pulse along the synapses of anti-Americanism that lurk in the nervous systems of even the most well-disposed non-Americans, including Canadians, because it is part of their self-definition.

I knew that, but I also knew that September 11 had changed something in me. While I understood how the president's words could be interpreted outside the U.S., my heart understood them differently. Watching the Twin Towers being attacked that day— watching in *my* city, New York—I awoke to a realization of how far I had traveled emotionally. For the first time in my long history of equivocation, I felt defensive about America as one feels about family and home when they are threatened. It shocked me differently from anything before. It made me want to examine what nationality, citizenship, and patriotism mean to me.

It forced me to consider what I believe in—and don't—and my choices. I am, after all, what my choices have made me, many of them oblique choices in my mind, distracted by various fevers—love, ambition, money, boredom, escape—induced me to move on, to start over.

For a long time I was a man with a nationality but no inner country; or a man with a country but no psychic nationality. Put otherwise: I was a man still looking for his country. And what did *country* mean? Literally a nation, or a culture, or those pieces of several I had assimilated and found congenial?

In a poem, "The City of Tomorrow," the poet laureate Billy Collins writes that it

> was not a place we would come to inhabit
> but a place that inhabited us.

For me, there was often a disconnect between the country I inhabited and the country that inhabited me. After September 11, the two came together.

Perhaps a Canadian who has made this psychological journey can explain the ambivalence America inspires. I grew up with a skepticism about the United States, a predisposition to disparage it, a certain cultural distaste. The source was two Canadian parents who each had one American parent, and therein lies a tale my brothers and I have only recently unraveled. I think it was a mild strain of the same virus that infects even America's friends, at its most innocent a sardonic humor, but a virus which, in less friendly places, can flare up murderously.

My ambivalence is the world's ambivalence in a sense, inspired by what is inspiring and disinterested in American behavior, with the luxury of being put off by what is sometimes excessive, crude, ungenerous, yet feeling deep empathy for an America chastened and scared by September 11.

· · ·

I became an American citizen in 1997. Unlike one's birth, chosen nationality is an examined nationality. Like chosen religion, it is part of the examined life. This freedom to choose one's nationality, one's religious affiliation, political attachments, sexual orientation and partners; whether to have children or not, whether to abort a child; the freedom of women to vote, to be educated, to take careers; the freedom to choose what one reads, to say what one thinks; to choose one's ethical standards, one's personal morality, are aspects of personal liberty that the United States has pioneered or greatly augmented in the last two centuries. They are precisely the freedoms abhorrent to religious fundamentalists here or abroad, Christian, Jewish, or Muslim.

I understood this well but I did not really get it, get it viscerally, until I watched those aircraft full of passengers—imagining their last seconds, their minds and hearts racing in terror—driven into the skyscrapers, then saw the ultimate despair of tiny figures leaping into space.

Seeing it suddenly vulnerable, I think I grasped in a new, almost mystical way, the true nature of the U.S.A.

Even if it sometimes appears conspicuously to lack Jefferson's "decent respect to the opinions of mankind"; even if Lincoln's "better angels" are not always in the ascendant; if it appears at times overweening, overbearing, and swaggering in its power, master of the universe; if it seems to outsiders to admire itself excessively; when it presumes uniquely to deserve God's blessing; even if, by comparison with others, it scants the poor to cosset the rich; the United States remains the most zealous promoter of democracy, the leading engine of world prosperity, the cockpit of social evolution and—though often compromised and embattled—the largest home of tolerance. It is, by and large, a force for good in the world. In a measure of ideals achieved, the glass is a lot more full than empty.

Thinking of Russia, Aleksandr Solzhenitsyn wrote, "When we say *nationality*, we do not mean blood, but always a spirit, a consciousness, a person's orientation of preferences."

Blood has never been the main American definition because her blood comes from everywhere: it has always been spirit, a consciousness, an orientation of preferences—and so it is for me. It just took me a long time to see it.

2

THE ROBIN IN THE SNOW

On the morning I was born, my mother said, snow was thick on the windowsill of her room and nestled in it was a live robin. Improbable? Well, it was January in Montreal, when migratory robins are supposed to be in Florida or Mexico, and not due this far north until April. But my mother swore by her story and gave me the nickname *Robin*, the old diminutive for Robert. So this was the bird of my destiny, his onboard computer out of whack, trying to bring the spring three months early. Certainly prophetic.

As children we greeted the first snowfall rapturously, ran out to plunge into it and make snowmen, then as we got older made snow forts with elaborate passages, waged huge wars with snowballs, went sledding until it was so dark we couldn't see the bottom of the hill. As a teenager, skiing became my wintertime passion.

At first, snow was emotionally exhilarating, transforming gray winter into fairyland, softening, muting, insulating sound, making nature more intimate, making you feel cozier. It turned me on. The first time I kissed a girl was in the snow.

Later, I began to envy my birthday robin his fall migration south and yearned for places that were not imprisoned by snow for six months of the year. No one looked more obsessively than I for the first hints of spring: little icicles on maple trees that showed the sap was running; tiny but discernible buds on bushes; crystalline thaw on southfacing snowbanks; the sun ascending as the solstice approached. And in me grew an abiding ambivalence not just about the climate, but about the country that climate governed: feelings of pleasure and oppression mixed. By my early twenties the sense of confinement the winters imposed had become a metaphor for my private view of the cultural environment in Canada.

Before and after World War II, we spent years in Ottawa, the coldest national capital after Ulan Bator, but my brothers and I grew up first in Halifax, where the maritime climate made for milder winters and cool summers, and I think of Halifax as my hometown.

It was my mother's birthplace. Her father, Warren Oxner, was descended from Swiss Protestants who settled near Lunenburg, Nova Scotia, in 1750. Her mother was Daisy Neely, a southern belle from Chattanooga, one of my two American grandparents.

In Halifax, Warren prospered as a dentist. They lived in a large stone house on Spring Garden Road, and Daisy cut a lively figure in Halifax society. They sent my mother, Peggy, to school in Switzerland, which gave Daisy a reason for regular trips to Europe.

In 1929, Bob MacNeil, representing Essex cars, turned up in Halifax. Seeing Peggy in the street, he picked a filling from a tooth and went to see her father the dentist, who liked the young man so much he invited him to dinner.

They were married in September 1929. A month later the Wall Street crash drove Essex cars out of business, and for three years Dad walked the streets of Montreal looking for work. Then, as the Great Depression really began to gnaw at Canadian life, he had another burden, a very sick child. I was born in 1931 and developed celiac, a disorder of the digestive system, causing chronic diarrhea and malnutrition. I spent much of the next two years in the hospital and, according to my grandmother Daisy, nearly died.

"Oh," she said in her dramatic way, "when I saw you in that hospital, you looked like one of the starving children in wartime. Your arms and legs were as thin as matchsticks and your belly was swollen out like this. I cried all the way back to Halifax in the train. I was sure I would never see you alive again."

Eventually, Alton Goldbloom, chairman of pediatrics at McGill University, suggested a diet heavy in bananas and I recovered. Bananas remained so important to my health that I took my own banana sandwiches to birthday parties until I was nine.

With no alternative for work, my father joined the Royal Canadian Mounted Police. A handsome and confident young man he was, with a flair for making a presence and a partiality to uniforms. Earlier service in the naval reserve led him into the Marine Section, then Canada's coast guard. He was quickly promoted and by the mid-1930s he had a master's ticket. He commanded one of the RCMP vessels based in Halifax, patrolling the East Coast and often chasing "rumrunners" loaded with illicit booze to evade U.S. prohibition.

When World War II began in September 1939, Dad and his

ship, *Laurier*, were seconded into the Canadian navy. Then for five years of war he commanded a series of convoy escort ships—two new corvettes, *Dauphin* and *Sorel*; a destroyer, *Columbia*; and the frigate *Wallaceburg*. For a daring rescue in mid-Atlantic he was decorated by the Norwegian government and later went to Buckingham Palace, where King George VI pinned on him the Order of the British Empire.

He had three sons now: my brother Hugh was born in 1934 and Michael in 1941. We grew up with a father often away at sea and our mother the effective parent.

In Halifax we lived in apartments, once briefly in a house, and by today's standards lived simply: no car, an icebox instead of a refrigerator, eking out the government paycheck from the flush moments just after payday to the lean ones at the end. "The end of the month" is a phrase rich with meaning from my childhood. But we were well fed and clothed, treated generously at Christmas and birthdays, and taken for months in the summer to rented cottages by the sea. Through the generosity of grandparents we had bicycles, BB guns, and chemistry sets. The low wages of the time permitted even families as close to the margin as ours to employ live-in maids, hearty girls from Newfoundland who soon found lonely sailors to cure their homesickness.

Anxious about our culture, my mother colluded with her friends to impose Saturday French lessons until we rebelled at the bad breath of the teacher. Worried that scrappy hockey games on the street made our skating ungraceful, she and other mothers paid for figure skating lessons. Concerned for our spiritual development, she forced us into blue suits on Sunday and marched us off to the Cathedral of All Saints. Some ungodly resistance caused me often to faint during the interminable communion services. I escaped by joining the choir, which I enjoyed and for which I got paid, ten cents a service. Since the anthems, chorales, and organ music of the Church of England drew on a rich tradition, it was also quite a musical education.

The theatrical, performance side of the choir duties awakened some predisposition in me to be onstage rather than in the audience. It may have been genetic: several MacNeil ancestors had been performers in one way or another, and the nascent show-off in me responded. I was eager for parts in school plays and, by my high school and college years, quite the serious actor. That, in turn, led me into broadcasting.

I attended public schools in Halifax, Le Marchant Street then Tower Road, through grade six, together with children of my mother's friends. It was a safe, disciplined environment. On our bikes, or by tramcar and on foot, we could explore most of the wartime city. Rougher areas, closer to the docks, we avoided, except when taken to the naval dockyard for visits to warships. The war was a constant presence. There were frequent blackouts and air raid drills. At twelve, I was trained by the St. John Ambulance Corps as a first aid messenger. When the sirens sounded, I would get out of bed and, with my gas mask and helmet, ride my bike to my reporting station. Beside our school they built an antiaircraft gun tower, and watching the men run drills on the guns was a wonderful distraction.

For a child the war did not feel extraordinary but normal, the world as we knew it. Your dad went off to work, taking ships out to sea to kill Germans, or to stop Germans from killing others. Other dads were in the army or air force, and some got killed. That was sad but it too seemed normal. The grown-ups talked about "the duration," but like any child's my life was *now*. Five years from eight to thirteen was an eternity, and I accepted anything in it as I did the snowfall or the fog around Halifax Harbor, the sound of foghorns, the deep notes of ships' whistles as they moved at night.

I was an enthusiastic Boy Scout, savvy enough about accumulating badges to become a King's Scout (the equivalent of Eagle Scout). We collected paper and metal in war salvage drives. One Saturday we found copies of *Esquire* magazine in an attic and hid them so we could gloat over the Vargas girls in lascivious privacy. That was foiled when the school principal saw them under our sweaters and, by the authority vested in him as guardian of our morals, took us to his office and gave us four tough whacks on each hand with the strap, the approved weapon of punishment in Halifax schools. The teachers, all women, used the strap for classroom misbehavior, some more enthusiastically than others. In school and at home we were drilled in good manners and grammatical speech, and in my home made to eat every scrap on our plates, even if that meant sitting for an hour over a plate of cold and disgusting liver.

I found ways of rebelling. At eight I stole twenty-five cents from my mother and bought firecrackers that I let off in the basement of a school I attended for a few months in Ottawa in 1939. I disliked the school and was delighted when they suggested I leave. For a few months I went to the Model School in downtown Ottawa until war broke out. The government commandeered the building and we moved to Halifax.

In Halifax, my friends and I raided fruit trees, shoplifted, and stole our parents' cigarettes. Or we'd go to distant stores and claim that our mothers had sent us to buy packets of five Sweet Caporals or British Consuls.

When there was frost but no snow we went skating on lakes across the Northwest Arm, an inlet from the Atlantic off Halifax Harbor, crossing in a rowboat ferry. Remembering her childhood, my mother sometimes put baked potatoes in the boots, which made the skates warm to put on and the potatoes delicious to eat in the frosty air. Picnics were a major entertainment on our own, or driving in my grandfather's Oldsmobile to more distant picnic spots along the coast.

It was he who took care of my easily decayed teeth, gently but insistently drilling and filling, and when the ordeal was over, always tipped me twenty-five cents—a fortune! He did all his lab work himself, and I spent absorbing hours watching him mix mercury and other ingredients for filling, softening wax sheets on his gas burner to make impressions, or constructing bridges or dentures. He taught me how to tell time and tie my shoelaces.

When we walked together I observed the way he managed the walking stick he always carried, moving it gracefully to match his stride. As it swung forward, he gripped the handle to freeze the motion for a beat, the tip poised in the air, then released it to touch the ground on every second pace. All my adult life, on serious walks I have carried a stick and swung it unconsciously as he did.

I heard of only one occasion when Warren was angry. Peggy, then ten or eleven, was attending the day school at the Sacred Heart convent and Daisy was away traveling. A dental patient mentioned casually that she had just seen Peggy wearing a lace veil and carrying a candle, going into the convent. Warren left the patient in the dental chair and, still in his white smock, ran the quarter mile along Spring Garden Road. He dashed into the chapel, where my mother was in a procession for first communion, grabbed her hand, and pulled her—lighted candle, veil, and all—out of there and back home. She was removed from the school. Warren was a Presbyterian, and no daughter of his was going to be lured into papism. My mother liked to tell the story, but all her life she yearned for the richer rituals of the Catholic Church and in her own devotions crept ever closer to the high church, Anglo-Catholic end of the Church of England.

Daisy had a birdlike manner, darting and flitting around and always pecking at me about something, sometimes humorously, often not, a prickly personality for a child to negotiate. To outsiders Daisy was an eccentric, trotting around Halifax with a wicker basket, taking sandwiches to shop girls she thought undernourished. During the war they sold their house and moved into a hotel, where Daisy embarrassed us by putting everything unfinished on the dining table (butter pats, rolls, pieces of cold chicken) in her crocodile bag for future meals in their rooms.

Socially, Daisy was a vivacious, even flirtatious, southerner. But for Peggy, her daughter, she had a sharp and wounding tongue. In their tormented relations, one or the other was continually trying to win me, the eldest grandchild, as confidant and ally. Daisy was constantly prying into our domestic economy, once famously rifling through our garbage when my mother was out, and finding a chicken carcass my mother swore had no meat on it.

"I don't understand it. I don't understand it!" Daisy would sit me down on one of the benches in the Public Gardens and, in a tragic voice, lecture me on what wastrels my parents were.

"A whole chicken! A whole chicken in the garbage. A *whole* chicken!" she'd say, jabbing my arm with her finger. "I pulled it out of the garbage. The girl had thrown it out. A family could have lived off that for a week. But Peggy doesn't care. She'll just charge another. She's never learned the value of money. She a fool with money." I had heard it so many times I had learned to nod my sympathy without giving away any vital information.

"Do you think that your grandfather and I would have what little we have today if we had thrown our money away like that? When we were first married and Warren was just starting his practice, we had nothing, absolutely nothing. We had no entertainments. At the end of one year we gave ourselves a treat. We went out to the nickelodeon, a film show, and it cost five cents. Five cents!"

My mother would say, "She has a wicked tongue that woman. She hurt me time and time again when I was young."

After the war when Daisy came, infrequently, to stay with us in Ottawa, she would exclaim, "How grandly you live, Peggy! Tomatoes out of season! I said to Mrs. Oland the other day, 'I'm going to Peggy's but I'll have to be careful not to put on weight because she serves such huge, rich meals! All the luxuries you can think of.' Mrs. Oland [one of the richest women in Halifax] says she never buys hothouse tomatoes but waits until they come into season."

This little speech always drove mother into a fury. With the first words the tiny harpoon would enter her flesh, and each calculated phrase implanted it further.

"Mother you stop it! You stop it!"

"Oh, Peggy dear, calm yourself," Daisy would say in a cooing voice. "How excitable you are!"

"I'm not excitable!" my mother would yell and slam out of the dining room to the kitchen to bang pots and swear, "I could kill that woman! I could cheerfully wring her neck!"

At this point Daisy altered tactics. Rising from the table, clutching her napkin, she would say in a hoarse whisper, "Please don't bother about me. I'll just go to my room."

Dad would say, "For heavens sake, Daisy, you have to eat something."

"My dear," said Daisy Sarah Bernhardt, leaning a little unsteadily on her chair. "Just a simple boiled egg and some bread and butter—later on." She would cough dryly, like someone with a flake of soda cracker caught in her throat.

Eventually my father began using that phrase to forestall the whole scene.

For Sunday lunch, having offered her a glass of sherry, Dad would say, with nothing apparent but his amiable concern, "Daisy, it's roast beef for lunch but I suppose you'd really prefer just a simple boiled egg and some bread and butter."

"What's that, dear? What's that?" she would ask, feigning deafness, bending forward, her sherry glass poised, the light reflecting off her spectacles.

Having to repeat it made Dad's irony a little heavy and obvious, then she became coquettish and arch. "Oh, heh, heh, heh. Isn't he cute? Isn't he cute? He's making fun of me! Isn't he cute! I'll never say another word about food in this house as long as I live."

These hostilities offer the only basis I can find for my mother's otherwise inexplicable anti-Americanism.

Daisy knew where the first mayflowers could be gathered and where to find Nova Scotia's elusive lady slippers. She worked hard for the war effort, helping to finance two mobile canteens shipped to England to feed workers and firefighters during the London Blitz. She had a secret source for chocolate bars, but insisted on keeping them in a drawer with mothballs so they were practically inedible.

Daisy could not have been more different from Emily Auburn, Dad's mother, a warm, affectionate woman, whom we visited about twice a year. As small children we would run to get into bed with her first thing in the morning because she loved to cuddle us and listen to our stories. We would never have done that with the decidedly uncuddly Daisy. Dad's father, Robert W. MacNeil, injured in World War I, lived in retirement in California, and another gentleman, George Fraser, resided in the Montreal house. That unorthodoxy was never discussed with us as children, but it was part of a larger puzzle we came to learn about only much later.

Visiting Montreal involved overnight train journeys; thrilling for small boys to sleep in the Pullman cars and get up for breakfast in a dining car that had starched white tablecloths, the shining cream jugs and sugar basins tinkling with the motion. If we stopped at a rural station in Quebec, I would wonder what the bundled-up locals, their breath steaming in the cold, would think of us, eating our porridge in such luxury.

From our frequent picnics and our summers by the ocean and from Dad's profession, the sea was a huge psychic presence—both actually and in the literature we were fed. With family lore reaching back to the Scottish Hebrides, our frequent gazing at the sea in all its moods gradually awakened the yearning to follow it to places of adventure and romance.

For Michael's christening in early 1942, Dad brought back seawater collected when his ship was in the Western Isles. The ceremony took place in the wardroom of HMCS *Dauphin*, the naval chaplain using the inverted ship's bell as a font, anointing our brother with the waters our ancestors had sailed. Pictures taken by a navy photographer made the newspapers. Dad had a flair for publicity. All corvette skippers chose personalized emblems for their gun turrets. *Dauphin*'s turret showed a Mountie astride a U-boat, riding it like a horse. That picture was widely published.

Dad was a passionate reader and collector of books. He drew

his further education and his dreams from books and determined to be a writer. That ambition got derailed by the Depression and the war, but his books were a constant in our homes, an ever-growing part of the interior decoration. In his absence, my mother read to us avidly, beginning with the traditional nursery rhymes, then A. A. Milne and on to Robert Louis Stevenson and Dickens.

Only now, considering my life, can I understand some of the emotional patterns that grew from my family experiences and affected my later behavior.

One was a reaction to female distress that might have been less sensitive if my father had been there more to absorb the burden of my mother's mood swings. At one pole she was the brisk, cheerful, capable homemaker and affectionate mother, whom we called Mum—she disliked the American *Mom*. That reasonable person receded when multiple anxieties overtook her, paramount among them her fear about Dad's survival in the highly dangerous life at sea. But it was augmented by her many layers of discontent, and I was a captive audience for tearful soliloquies on her loneliness, money worries, her anger at Dad's financial irresponsibility; suspicion of his philandering, annoyance at his heavy drinking; her feelings of social inferiority compared to childhood friends; plus the ongoing narrative of the psychological warfare with her mother. This all poured out in a continuous and repetitive stream. It induced in me a reaction similar to Dad's when he was home: initially comforting, then impatient for anything to tamp it down, manage it, avoid the bigger storm, hope this one will soon blow over. Sometimes it simply angered me and we got into serious fights, whose precise causes I can't now remember. But the pattern grew in me to avoid such scenes at all costs—and that was not a good preparation for life.

3

THERE'LL ALWAYS BE AN ENGLAND

*I*n early summer 1940, Halifax schoolchildren were massed outdoors to sing patriotic songs for a Victory Bond drive. We were all in white, mingling our reedy voices in songs from World War I and the stirring new hymn to Britishness, "There'll Always Be an England." My eyes were stinging and my chest bursting with too much feeling. It was the first time I felt the emotion of patriotism.

All our emotive paraphernalia and symbolism then were British. The king and queen looked down on us from pictures in our schoolrooms. The king was on our money and postage stamps. Canada's flag was the British red ensign, with the Union Jack in the upper corner and a shield of symbols for the provinces. My father's ships were known as His Majesty's Canadian Ships and flew the white ensign of the Royal Navy. In school we disassembled the Union Jack with three-fold cutouts demonstrating the union of England, Scotland, and Wales. In the Canadian Boy Scouts we learned that flying the Union Jack upside down was a signal of distress.

So, embedded wherever in one's core memories patriotism resides, the Union Jack is the flag that stirred my youthful soul.

Canada did not get its own flag until a belated wave of nationalist spirit surfaced in the 1960s. Adopted in 1965, it is younger than the logos of some corporations and carries for me the same aura of graphic-design-studio contrivance. For an NBC documentary entitled *Québec Oui—Ottawa Non,* I stood on Parliament Hill in Ottawa describing the competition to design the new flag. One at a time I showed the half dozen finalists, each a variation of maple leaves and the colors red, white, and blue. They were all pleasant and the government might as profitably have chosen one as another. The winner looks perky on the tails of Air Canada jets or the gas stations of PetroCanada. It still looks faintly opportunistic flying over the Parliament buildings. In me it evokes no patriotic resonance, but of course it does for children growing up now, watching Canadian Olympic medalists wave it. And the red ensign had to go; it proclaimed too late into the century a message of lingering colonial connection, of national adolescence unnaturally prolonged, a flag of dominion, not nationhood.

The person I acknowledged as my leader, the personification of our identity, was not the prime minister in Ottawa (who happened to be named King) but The King in London. We did not gather by the radio to hear Mackenzie King, the introverted, matronly bachelor who was our prime minister; who might, in Victorian drag, have passed for the Old Queen herself. When there was a radio event important enough to the family to get my attention too, it concerned the kings—George V, Edward VIII, and George VI—who reigned in my first ten years.

I was five when George V died, and the day of his funeral is my first memory of any political occasion. On a chill, sleeting day in January, my father, much moved by the event, took me along. They fired a lengthy salute from artillery guns on Citadel Hill in Halifax, the concussions splitting the winter sky as we stood sheltered in a doorway on the north side of the great hill. In my memory, the frozen streets around us were deserted, as though only my father had the emotion to come and pay his respects.

Now I know it was a very real sentiment of loyalty that moved him but also his itching to be where things were happening, and that itch was infectious. On that day, London was where what mattered was happening and, here in this frozen outpost of empire, our hearts were tied to those doings.

That is the essence of the colonial psychology with which I grew up. It did not matter that Mackenzie King was doing sly things to make Canada more independent. It wouldn't have done to trumpet them. The slyer the better. Too much independence smacked of republicanism and the bad taste the Americans (always "the Americans") had shown by thumbing their noses at Britain. I never heard any sentiment applauding Canadian assertiveness to London. What was applauded was loyalty, faith, fealty.

It was London we listened to, my parents hushed and anxious, when Edward VIII abdicated to marry Mrs. Simpson. It was from London that the shortwave brought us the painful, stuttering rhetoric of his brother, George VI, then, as World War II advanced, the thrilling voice of Winston Churchill. The news that penetrated my consciousness was the BBC News from London. Sixty years later I can still remember the name of the news reader, Derek Prentice.

Books were even more powerful an influence. Through my mother's reading and my own afterward, I was steeped in English sensibility, humor, character, places. So powerful was this feeding of my imagination that English and Scottish landscapes acquired a poetic value our prosaic Canadian landscapes did not have. Our scenery, of course some of the most glorious on earth, did not have the magic patina of having been written about, of having the emotions of characters in books lend it sentiment. That imagined lack in turn invested British children with a glow of romance. Such was the heightened reality engendered in me by much-loved books. We have all felt it. But if the feelings are always directed outside your own country, where will a sense of your country come from? The answer gradually crystallized: to have an exciting life, to have adventures, to feel the existential thrill, you had to be something else, somewhere else. This accumulated envy of boys more adventitiously born than I became a sensibility. For some part of my young life, I actually longed to be English.

In my mother's definitions of worth, the credential that always carried the most force was the label "Made in England." The "proper thing," the "real thing," "the good stuff" came from England. "Look at that," my mother would say, fingering a sweater or a scarf in a shop, "that's real English wool!"

"Real English" anything usually required sacrifice because worshiping at this altar meant paying more. They were dues to British loyalty exacted long after the British had stopped caring about anything except their balance of payments and making a quid.

If she could, my mother served English biscuits with cheese, and sweet English biscuits with tea; English tea, and brewed the English way, the pot preheated. They drank English gin and preferred English marmalade, pipe tobacco, clothes, and shoes. "The English shoes are so sensible. . . . I think the Queen Mother dresses so beautifully. . . . I do love this thin English china, I hope I can replace the cups I broke. . . ." My mother's litany of yearning for goods that came from Britain was almost religious, an ache of loyalty to supposed values of craftsmanship, design integrity, and quality.

Her obsession embraced not just goods but attitudes and values. She adored English speech and manners, their houses and gardens, the way they brought up their children, even the way they cut boys' hair. "I hate the way these barbers shave you up the back of the neck and around your ears, and make that disgusting swirl over your forehead. I love the way they do it in England. It makes the shape of the boys' heads so much more attractive." And in reading A. A. Milne, she would stop to moon over Christopher Robin's haircut.

And manners: "English children have such beautiful manners. They really know how to bring them up. You boys are becoming such roughnecks. And the way they talk! They don't swallow their words and mumble. . . ." and so on, an endless incantation, as though saying her prayers to the god of Englishness might, if we all strove to be worthy, make us better people.

I felt a leap of recognition when V. S. Naipaul's Mr. Biswas cycled to the cricket match in Trinidad, imagining himself English in his suit, his bicycle clips, umbrella, and flat fifty tin of English cigarettes. It is a postcolonial truism how such imitated values distort or stifle the growth of real identity, regardless of race or color.

Naipaul gave me a double flash of recognition because I was briefly a passionate cricketer. In the schoolyard in Halifax we played baseball, but during my high school years I attended two English-style schools, Rothesay in New Brunswick and Ashbury in Ottawa, where cricket was played. It was the only team sport at which I showed any talent and I loved it. I found sensual pleasure in all aspects of the game, the look and feel of a new cricket ball, gleaming cherry red in its fresh varnish, its faint stickiness and the proud lines of fresh stitching, like a glue to the bowler's fingertips. The bats, laminated willow and ash, were ingeniously soft and flexible yet mechanically strong, and produced a variety of pleasing sounds when bat met ball in different strokes in different thicknesses of summer air. I enjoyed the courage it took to catch a hard drive with bare hands—no fielders' gloves in cricket—or to stand a few feet from a determined batsman in hopes of intimidating him and forcing an error, or if he blasted one straight at you, somehow catching it. I broke two fingers that way and, I suppose, somewhere in my lower consciousness, felt English doing it.

I may have missed signals of Canadian pride that my parents sent and I failed to receive. But if I missed them, they could not have been very determined signals.

Now here was a paradox, because my father was, after the war, once again that quintessentially Canadian thing, a Mountie. On ceremonial occasions he wore the scarlet tunic and Stetson that say "Canada" everywhere. Because he looked the part so splendidly, he was the officer they chose to escort President Truman and Winston Churchill on visits to Ottawa. So why, with this potent symbol of national identity living under our roof, was my sense of the nation so attenuated? Because he was somewhat ambivalent about it himself? Because it represented failure to do what he really longed to do with his life? Because in my mother's eyes the RCMP was socially inferior to the other services?

My father was proud of what he achieved in the wartime navy—and deserved to be—but how difficult it is to disentangle the strands of loyalty, to find where Canadian pride (the little "Canada" shoulder patch in gold on his otherwise British uniform) was distinct from pride in being part of the larger British effort, from pride in British recognition of that service. The old story, like the awards for valor (valour): what was especially meritorious in a Canadian was decided in London.

In World War I, Canadians initially were thrilled to be serving king and empire. As their losses mounted and their heroic fighting was noted, Ottawa demanded and won separate identity and command autonomy for Canadian divisions, to throw off the complacent anonymity of "imperial forces." With fifty thousand dead out of a total population of only 8 million, Canada earned that autonomy and with it an important step in national self-awareness. J. W. Pickersgill, a witty and much-loved minister in governments of the 1950s and '60s, told me of his own service in the trenches in World War I. "We went over as British, we came back Canadians."

Patiently, stubbornly, sometimes deviously, Canada added to that independence in the 1920s and '30s, a grain of national self-assertion at a time. Canadian governments knitted a revolution so quiet, so decent, so well-behaved, that it was barely noticeable. But none of that was paraded to us in our school days. No history teachers ever added up all the gestures of self-determination and said, You see how our nationhood is growing? It was an unmentioned subject, certainly no nourishment to psychological nationalism.

Some Canadians, looking now for ways to pump up national consciousness, bemoan Canada's weakness in the hero-creation that comes so easily to Americans. In Bertolt Brecht's *Galileo*, one character, Andrea, says, "Unhappy the land that has no heroes." To which Galileo replies, "No, unhappy the land that *needs* heroes."

I mentioned that line to Allan Gottlieb, a former Canadian ambassador to Washington, who said: "Well, Canadians can have other people's heroes." Which says a lot.

There was a lack of mythmaking in the Anglo-Canadian psyche because our imaginations were nourished by the mother country's myths for so long that we neglected our own. Americans took care of that with Oedipal verve: by taking arms against Britain, their story became instant myth, with heroes like George Washington mythologized before they were even dead.

In World War II the Canadian navy was a major player in winning the battle to keep the Atlantic sea-lanes open, but Canadian deeds were not celebrated in the same high-publicity anthems that were sung of British or American naval exploits. Going to the movies about the war, Canadians had to be satisfied with vicarious pride through American and British actors. Thus we saw Noel Coward's *In Which We Serve*, and Nicholas Monsarrat's *The Cruel Sea*, and tried to thrill with empathy as we said, "That's what it was like for Dad." Growing up in a cultural economy too small to boast its own wartime epics meant that some nourishment for our national identity had to be supplied by other, richer cultures. The movies Canadians flocked to see—often with Canadian actors like Raymond Massey playing Americans—were the movies made in Hollywood or London. When you see only black-and-white photographs you imagine the color. When Canadians saw American and British movies about World War II, they imagined the Canadian relevance.

In me, these many factors contributed to one conviction which grew like an irrefutable axiom: if it matters, it is happening somewhere else.

. . .

I grew up in a nation trying to build a distinctive culture in an environment that constantly threatens extinction, physical from the north, and political/cultural from the south. Each fear in its own way reinforces the other. The inhospitality of the northern climate induces Canadians to drift southward, and the magnet of American material prosperity and opportunity reinforces that urge. Yet the fear of being swallowed, ingested by the American Leviathan, makes Canadians draw back, shrinking from the smothering embrace, to find a source of national pride and identity in overcoming the natural human fear of perishing in frozen wastes.

Peter Gzowski, the late, beloved Canadian radio host, once ran a competition to complete the sentence, "*As Canadian as . . .*" The winner suggested, "*As Canadian as possible under the circumstances.*"

I had my own small example as a child stamp collector. Flushed with the generosity of the American consul, I quickly ran into the usual problem. Our stamp albums, printed in the U.S., had hundreds of places and illustrations for American stamps, too few for everything else, and almost nothing for Canada. U.S. cultural imperialism rampant even in 1942!

So I concentrated on a few British possessions because the issues had beauty and coherence. Kenya and Tanganyika, Rhodesia and Nyasaland, Trinidad and Tobago all showed, not mustachioed and ephemeral politicians, but beautiful scenes of African wildlife or Caribbean flora. Since the scenes often remained the same when the king changed, I knew where I was with British stamps. As a stamp collector, I was a fond little imperialist.

My stamp prejudice may have been nourished by the other side of my mother's Anglophilia—her negative feelings about Americans. I can only guess where this came from, perhaps from the tensions with her mother. Once when one of us pointed out that her own mother was American, she retorted, "No, she's a southerner!" But it was always in the air, her sniffiness about the U.S. that covered almost all aspects of life and manners.

An essential component of the Canadian personality when I was becoming aware of the world, it persists today and is seldom treated honestly. Canadians tend to look at the United States through two ends of the telescope alternately: close up and sympathetically, distantly and critically—overmagnifying and belittling.

One strain of the virus I heard constantly during World War II was a half-joking, half-serious disparagement of the American military. It held that American forces were spoiled, sloppy, undisciplined, and not, man for man, the fighters Canadians were, or British, or others. It held that Americans eventually succeeded by sheer numbers, that they sheltered behind massive matériel superiority.

"Have you ever watched Americans march?" my father would say. "They slouch along, shuffle along. Their backs aren't straight, they hang their heads, they don't swing their arms." Foot drill, impeccable marching in rigid lines, each man stiff with pride and discipline, ranked high in Dad's military values. Sloppiness, slouching, round-shouldered stepping along instead of striding out, betokened an undisciplined force.

"The American troops are always whining," my mother said. "In the movies they're always moaning about home, and mother, and not getting mail. Why can't they control themselves like the British when there's a war on?"

As a youngster I thought "battle fatigue" was an American phenomenon, because the Americans were soft, not battle-hardened like our troops. Peggy again: "You don't hear about British soldiers crying and saying they're too upset to fight."

There were sneering references left over from World War I—when Americans fought one year to four for Canadians, reinforced by the late U.S. entry into our war—that Americans watched while British and Commonwealth troops did the hard stuff and then, with overwhelming strength, came in to claim the victory. The prejudice about the late U.S. entry in the second war persisted despite Roosevelt's Lend-Lease program, from which my father personally benefited. He was given command of one of the fifty U.S. destroyers transferred to the British and Canadian navies before Pearl Harbor. The World War I four-stacker USS *Columbia* became HMCS *Columbia*.

As children we sang a verse from the World War I song "Mademoiselle from Armentières,"

> The Americans said they won the war,
> Parlez-vous.
> The Americans said they won the war,
> Parlez-vous.
> The Americans said they won the war,
> But the British had done it years before,
> Inky-dinky, parlez-vous.

There was resentment of the publicity machine that promoted American achievements; partly innate Canadian distaste for American hyperbole, but also feeding perpetual Canadian frustration at being overlooked, prompting remarks like, "Look at that. You'd think bloody James Cagney was winning the god-damned war all by himself!"

Once during the Reagan years my mother, then in her eighties, called me in New York from Halifax and said, "Oh, Rob, I do wish the Americans would stop boasting so much!" It is a sentiment many Canadians would recognize. It is in the American nature to thump its chest, and in the Canadian nature to resent it. Canadians want to boast themselves but feel it is in bad taste. Canadians would love to be boasted about, if only someone else would do it. It is both modesty and an affectation of modesty. It is mildly neurotic. I recognize it in myself.

During the Gulf War in 1991 the *Toronto Globe and Mail* ran a story about a Canadian doctor, Richard Heinzl, who was helping in a Kurdish refugee camp. Dr. Heinzl rejected any suggestion that he was a hero, "It's not Canadian to be a hero. I just want to be a Canadian and do my job." The newspaper made that its quote of the day. An American friend, Robert Kotlowitz, was visiting us in Nova Scotia and he said the false modesty of the statement made him sick. Kotlowitz was a soldier in World War II and wrote a most affecting memoir, *Before Their Time*, a study in antiheroics.

But it is fundamental to Canadians to identify themselves partly by what they are not. One way of presenting yourself as Canadian in the rest of the world is to say, I am not an American, because the rest of the world often fails to see the difference in accent, clothes, comportment.

In my family there was prejudice at an absurdly trivial level about the U.S. Navy. "They all look like accountants," my mother would say of American officers, "with their glasses and mustaches." Canadian, like Royal Navy, officers could wear beards but no mustaches, and seldom did an executive officer appear in uniform wearing glasses. A monocle was ridiculed but tolerated. "They don't look like proper naval officers. And their bottoms are too big!" Thus, Peggy MacNeil on the might of the U.S. Navy, because she did not approve of the cut of the American officers' jackets. U.S. officers were ridiculed for wearing plastic rain covers over their white summer hats. "French safes" (meaning condoms), they were uncharitably called.

It was a source of pity or condescension that American ships were "dry," no liquor in the wardrooms, no rum for the seamen, the rum an eighteenth-century relic then thought still essential to the fighting spirit of the British and Canadian navies.

There was even criticism that the hulls of American warships were welded, not riveted as were British ships, on grounds that welded ships were weaker. In fact, welding was an advance in shipbuilding, making for greater productivity and is the standard today. But it was another of those little niggling prejudices that will be snatched at to feed a deeper emotional hunger—in this case Canada's need for recognition and identity—and ambivalence about where her fate ultimately lay, with Britain or with the U.S.

So my early identity was implanted with a thousand little cultural seeds, all saying one way or another, We're British, not American. The seeds covered almost every aspect of living. My parents disliked what they called "bratty kids," and it was understood that most Americans had them because you saw them in movies and heard them on the radio and occasionally met them. Bratty meant whining, spoiled, overindulged, undisciplined, disrespectful—you name it—intrusive, demanding, uncooperative, not knowing their place, smart-alecky with grown-ups.

The American voice was another peeve of my mother's. She

described it with words like *twangy, nasal, loud*, and constantly urged us to "modulate your voice." She never actually said, "Talk like the English," but never missed a chance to make her preference clear. "I do love the way they talk—even the children—it's so soothing to listen to." One of the nicest things she could say about anybody was "She has the nicest speaking voice—not like an American at all." When I first came to the U.S. with short-lived pretensions as an actor, I deliberately modified the Canadian diphthong "ou," pronounced in Nova Scotia so that *out* rhymed with *boat*. When I shed that regionalism and began a lifelong struggle to make *ou* sound like *shout*, my mother ridiculed it until her death. She would exaggerate so that it came out almost like Eliza Doolittle's Cockney *Ah-ow-ooh!* "Why are you trying to sound so American?" she'd ask.

Other components were often articulated: Americans were too interested in money, had too much of it, and threw it around ostentatiously. It assumed that if we had had money, we would have spent it more discreetly, more tastefully, and altogether un-Americanly. Among a class of Canadians there was a different attitude to consumption that affects me still, a desire to consume inconspicuously.

So these cultural biases accumulated into a composite stereotype of people who did not know how to fight, dress, speak, bring up their children, had too much money, and boasted too much into the bargain. Otherwise they were wonderful!

These home attitudes were reinforced at school, for example, in the way history was taught, particularly history relating to the division of British North America. The approving emphasis was on the Loyalists, who opposed the Revolution and the privations these fifty thousand middle-class people suffered in removing themselves to Canada.

In my early schooling we formed a picture of those who made the Revolution as a disreputable mob. There was no suggestion that anyone in Nova Scotia had sympathized with the Revolution; I did not learn for decades that this fourteenth colony had sent delegates to the Continental Congress, that there was revolutionary sentiment but it was stifled by the presence of large British garrisons.

Nor did I learn (and few Americans are taught) how much sympathy for the colonists there was in Britain, how closely debated the issue was, although the king's party in Parliament inevitably prevailed. There is a revealing passage in George Otto Trevelyan's history of the American Revolution, describing the stagecoach journey from Bristol to London of several Tory refugees who had just landed from America. Expecting to be cheered for their loyalty, instead they're chastised by fellow passengers for deserting their compatriots in the colonies. My reading this eventually led to a special BBC/PBS program "Goodbye America," made for July 4, 1976, dramatizing the last debate in the British Parliament before the Declaration of Independence. We covered it as though a current news story, with reports from the colonies, Tom Paine's talks with the troops, and background pieces on the Boston Tea Party, Bunker Hill, Lexington, and Concord.

. . .

But if my patriotism and my literary imagination soared on wings made in Britain, there was another paradox: most of the popular culture I consumed was American: radio programs, movies, comic books, and popular songs. I was addicted to *Amos 'n Andy, Fibber McGee, The Green Hornet, The Lone Ranger*, and *The Shadow*, every scrap of the popular ether I could plead, cajole, steal radio time to hear.

Even more evocative emotionally, because they resonate to this day, were the popular American songs that swamped Canadian airwaves. When I recall any one, I touch such a chord of feeling that an entire day, with all its emotional variety, floods back. I'm talking of songs as innocent as "Rum and Coca Cola," "Swingin' on a Star," "Don't Fence Me In," "Accentuate the Positive," or as powerful as "I'll Be Seeing You," "Oh What a Lovely Way to Spend an Evening," "Sentimental Journey," and "As Time Goes By."

These songs seemed to go into quite a different place in my psychic sound library than the British songs we knew. "There'll Always Be an England," "The White Cliffs of Dover," "We'll Meet Again," "Wish Me Luck as You Wave Me Goodbye," which went into the British patriotism compartment.

So my sentimental education had at least two personalities: the British stirring to duty and sacrifice, and the American, romantic and funny.

. . .

My father's attitude to the U.S. was milder and better informed than my mother's. His wide reading embraced all modern American writers, with particular devotion to Hemingway. He adored Damon Runyon and during the war, signaling to other ships, used Runyon characters as nicknames for his buddies. In one job he worked with the FBI, when the Mounties broke a spy ring operating from the Soviet embassy. Later he was the RCMP's liaison to Hollywood and came back with hilarious stories of his efforts to give future movies about the Mounties some realism. He stayed in touch through the Sunday *New York Times*, which he would go off to buy through winter snow or summer heat. In short, apart from his military prejudices, he got a kick out of Americans. He would say in mock perplexity about almost anything, "What people these Americans!" And behind his curiosity must have been his own father living in California, my other American grandparent.

Dad introduced me to George Gershwin, giving me *Rhapsody in Blue* in an album of 78s on my sixteenth birthday. The music had a huge effect on me. It was so impertinent, deliciously mocking of everything that was disciplined and prosaic in my life, the flat-stale-and-unprofitableness of teenage existence. It insinuated into my mind the notion that there was a life for people who could be iconoclastic, witty, unconventional, passionate, lyrical, daring. I made myself a little drunk listening to those discs again and again—Oscar Levant and the Paul Whiteman Orchestra. The orgasmic sentimentality of the climactic theme, the opening clarinet's jazz wail, were fresh to me and yet the emotions they stirred felt like things I knew in my bones. I drank it up, spirit, atmosphere, and voice.

Americans might be everything my mother said, but if Gershwin was Americanism, it was powerfully seductive.

What happened in my impressionable years is that Canada became the battleground for my sense of national identity, a psychological war for my soul, fought on Canadian soil. The combatants were my severely Anglophile mother, pumping me full of Englishness, and the broad popular culture beckoning from America.

In a tiny way, that struggle mirrored the wider struggle that was happening in Canada in the years of my growing up: where did her destiny lie—with Britain or with the United States? In his novel *World of Wonders*, the Canadian writer Robertson Davies observed, "The Canadians knew themselves to be strangers in their own land, without being at home anywhere else." For years I was haunted by that thought. I was sure it applied to me.

4

THE LAND OF INDULGENCE

*M*y first actual taste of the U.S. came in 1952, when I was twenty-one.

All through my teenage years my father expected that I would go into the Canadian navy as a career. With no other clear ambition, I accepted that, but by the age of sixteen I had been bitten by the acting bug and my interest in the theater gradually displaced the navy. It was an unconscious process because even when I took the naval entrance exams after my high school graduation, I expected to pass and enter the naval college, Royal Roads, in British Columbia. My subconscious must have been at work because I failed the algebra paper and was rejected by the navy, producing big gloom in the family.

To recover, with help from grandparents, I enrolled at Dalhousie University in Halifax and joined the University Naval Training Division (UNTD), the Canadian equivalent of the ROTC. Money earned from weekly parades and a summer with the navy would pay my tuition, and I could either reapply to the naval college or emerge with a degree and a reserve commission. In the first year at Dalhousie, I did attend the weekly parades, but the theater kept drawing me in and I appeared in several plays, including *Othello*. After my performance as Cassio, a producer for the Canadian Broadcasting Corporation came backstage and offered me work in live radio drama. So I became a regular in a little stock company of professional actors. We did modern dramas and long series for schools, including *Treasure Island* and *The Count of Monte Cristo*.

I dutifully spent the first summer in naval training, but by the second year of college I wanted out. That infuriated Dad, who said I was disgracing the service in which he had served. But I followed my own bent, cramming in as much acting as I could at college and with CBC radio.

In the regional finals of the Dominion Drama Festival, I won the best actor award. So I was quite full of myself when my second year of college ended, until the acting petered out for the summer. I got a part-time announcing job with the CBC, but it offered too few hours to support me. I worked briefly as a warehouseman for the power company until they found me incompetent and let me go. I was a census taker for two weeks, but then the summer grew very lean. One day I was reduced to lugging all my empty milk bottles to the grocery for the refunds (about sixty cents) to buy sweet potatoes, on which I survived for several days. I fell so far behind in my rent that I had to pay off twenty-two weeks by painting, with a fellow indigent, the entire exterior of a large Victorian rooming house. My girlfriend got fed up and threw me over for a guy, ironically, in the University Naval Training Division.

Then in September I heard of a job as an all-night disc jockey in a commercial radio station and grabbed it. I was an unlikely performer in that role, my taste in music now running to Mozart and my concessions to pop music limited to Gershwin, Broadway show tunes, and the Benny Goodman Carnegie Hall jazz concert of 1938. Necessity forced some rapid reeducation, and soon I could affect familiarity with all the current *Hit Parade* stars— Frank Sinatra, Dinah Shore, Patti Page, Teresa Brewer, Sarah Vaughan, Jo Stafford, and Rosemary Clooney. Hence further immersion in American popular culture. There was an LP by Gordon Jenkins entitled *Manhattan Tower*, a sentimental essay delivered over syrupy music about a man yearning to live in a New York apartment. Trash, I thought, but it must have spoken to my own desires because I played it repeatedly.

I dropped out of college and burned the candle at both ends that winter. I got a regular part in a CBC radio daytime serial. Several days a week I would finish my disc jockey slot at 7 A.M., have breakfast, walk home to the room I rented, sleep till eleven, then go to the CBC studios. My internal rhythms kept me from sleeping in the afternoons. Most evenings I would be rehearsing a stage play or a radio drama for the CBC, always breaking off early to be ready for the all-night shift. I had no social life outside this regime and I was always tired.

When a chance came to enlarge my acting experience in the U.S. for the summer of 1952, I quit my job, parked my books with friends, and headed south in a 1934 SS100, an early Jaguar worth three hundred dollars. I left with a Zenlike sense of freedom from material burdens or consequences, an eager sponge for new experience. When the car broke down on a lonely highway in Maine, I sat unanxious by the side of the road until help came along, as it did. When I thought motels would too soon deplete my small hoard of cash, I slept in the car.

Each new mile of my progress down U.S. 1 threw the life I had left behind in Nova Scotia into starker contrast. The deeper I penetrated into New England, the elm trees in the old towns grew taller, the houses progressively grander, the density of wealth more apparent. I was taken with the thicker sandwiches and the endless catechism about what particular kind of bread, ham, cheese, and accessories I wanted. I reveled in the delis and package stores, with no stuffy obstacles to buying beer and wine.

Everything—air, temperature, and social atmosphere—felt softer and more indulgent. It suggested that money is to be spent, don't worry, there'll be more money. Put off the garments of guilt and self-denial. The real puritan came to puritan country where the puritans had become hedonists. In Canada, I had felt that consumption had to be explained to oneself, rationalized, justified against need, excused, apologized for. Consumer spending in my pinched attitude was a reluctant act, made against the grain, swimming upstream against the current of my conscience.

An American friend encountered years later, asked why she needed to buy something she coveted, responded hotly: "What's *need* got to do with it?" In the U.S., to spend was to float with the current, with much lighter garments of guilt or calculation. The shops are full, so buy! It was a little like my parents when they were "in the cash" just after payday. Irish insouciance and the devil may care. That was the feeling of my first American days: have what you like; anyone can have what he likes. I felt the release of having slipped the hairshirt of duty and self-denial.

It contrasted dramatically with the spirit of unavailability, of restriction; of the too-meager population in Nova Scotia to make commerce hum like this and to create the jobs to run it. No wonder, I thought, generations of Nova Scotians had escaped to "the Boston states."

The warmer air, the soft humid nights on the beaches south of Plymouth, the languorous feeling on my skin, was my first experience of self-indulgence associated with going south; what the Loyalists going north must have surely regretted, or gritted themselves not to: balmier air, sometimes too hot, sultrier, tastier, spicier air.

My senses felt awakened, my nostrils enlivened by headier smells than I was used to: the Turkish hint in American tobacco, spicier food, more aromatic coffee, more obvious sweat and deodorants to suppress it, of soaps and perfumes. God knows, there were plenty of pungent smells in Halifax—sea, ships, tar, oil, fish. Yet, the ethnic minestrone of America, so unlike Canada in the early '50s, generated a spicy, garlicky, herbal potpourri absent or discouraged in Canada's white porcelain airs. There must, I thought, be a different sensuality in a colder climate, fewer outdoor smells in the paler summer.

I blossomed a little that summer in Massachusetts. The people were as welcoming and relaxed as the climate. Although everyone worked hard in the Priscilla Beach Theater, the atmosphere was easy and informal. I was the only non-American, so faintly exotic, with my stiffer manners and more formal speech. Even informally I never dropped my "g's". Their gentle ridicule made me quickly try to change my "ou" sound, but I was put into character parts because I sounded vaguely English to them. I knew a little more history, more Shakespeare than some of them, but a good deal less about life.

The professional acceptance was heady, but the personal message gratified another desire. They unstarched me. There were young women from all over the U.S., quite different from the girls I knew in Canada—more forward, more candid, meeting me more than halfway. There was a different kind of openness, less defensive, an open door to friendship, on different levels. I began to adapt and feel at home.

I picked up small habits to fit in, smoking Chesterfields, enjoying the small pleasurable skill quickly learned of opening the soft pack (Canadian cigarettes came in hard boxes) and tapping out the cigarette. Just to be able to do that made me feel American. I felt worldly with the Chesterfield burning on the edge of the makeup table as I applied the character disguises I had a talent for producing—various mustaches and other devices to make me older and different. I shook off inhibitions as I discarded the tweeds and gray flannels of my square college wardrobe for the chinos and polo shirts of my new American friends.

Yet I did not discard all of my prejudices. My roommate was a schoolteacher from Ohio, using the summer to hone his dramatic skills. He arrived in a new Plymouth, which he was buying on time, and it gave me mixed emotions. My exotic Jag, long hood, huge chrome headlamps, wire wheels, knock-off hubs, spent the summer in a field. Attracted by its glamour, the girls wanted rides, and a crowd would push it to start the engine, sputtering and roaring in its sick antique way. My roommate's Plymouth, humming about noiselessly, of course always starting, did all our necessary errands. Nevertheless, I pitied him for tying himself and—horror of horrors, going into debt—harnessing his soul to the mass consumer society.

That was what the materialist culture did to you if you didn't watch out, I told myself. It sucked you into a lifetime of material acquisition and robbed you of the freedom to follow your own compass. Yet he had reliable, comfortable transportation and I had a piece of romantic junk. Unable to afford another generator (rare, chain-driven, to be imported from England), when a local mechanic drooled over the Jag I sold it to him for sixty-seven dollars.

Looking back fifty years, I find it remarkable that if I had absorbed anything of my mother's view of Americans, it evaporated instantly on meeting and working with them. It would strike me that anti-Americanism is often a reaction to an abstract United States or Americans seen from afar: it seldom arises in dealing with real Americans personally. What generates the negative feelings deserves examination, especially now as the only superpower, or hyperpower as the French called America, it inspires even more hostility.

What also intrigues the political animal in me is to remember that 1952 was a key presidential election year, with Republicans desperate to end twenty years of Democratic rule. That summer millions of Americans were transfixed by the conventions that nominated Dwight Eisenhower and Adlai Stevenson. Yet I can't recall anyone ever mentioning it, so the cocoon around our theatrical community must have been very tight. Or perhaps it was just my own self-absorption, working long hours, often mounting two plays in a week.

At the end of the summer the management offered me a job for a winter season at the Brattle Theater in Cambridge, and we began rehearsing *Gaslight*. I had learned about half my lines when they told us the season had fallen through. So, with sixty-seven dollars from the sale of my car, I got a lift with some other actors and went to conquer New York City. I existed for ten days on grapes and the generosity of a girlfriend while I went the rounds of casting producers. Then, quite unexpectedly, an inner voice told me that acting was not my game. I was crossing Times Square on a hot September day, my tweed jacket too warm for the season, when this voice declared that I would make a lousy actor; I wasn't cut out to shop myself around like a commodity; I was meant to be a writer, the cool one behind the scenes, and a writer needed more education. No conviction, no decision in my life has ever been clearer. I believed this voice, borrowed the bus fare, and went back to Canada.

To enter the U.S. to work I had immigrated, sworn that I was not a communist or coming for immoral purposes, and I had a green card. If I had found work as an actor, the voice might not have spoken and I probably would have stayed in the U.S. I went back to Canada to regroup. Returning to Ottawa where my parents lived, I got a radio job and enrolled for night courses at Carleton College (now University).

I returned to New York occasionally to visit friends from the summer. Their freedom to live, however humbly, to experience day by day this pulsing city, filled me with envy and ambition. Just to walk down upper Broadway, near Columbia where they lived, was to be reminded of everything Canada lacked.

There were bookstores of every possible kind, open into the steamy nights and on Sundays. In Ottawa, the Canadian capital, there were precisely two bookstores at the time, the books all written it seemed by non-Canadians and the prices discouragingly steep. They were not open on Sundays. Nothing was open on Sunday, and Canada's blue laws prevented any Sunday newspapers. Just to see the stacks of the Sunday *New York Times* piling up on

Saturday nights at the newsstands, to lug it home, to spend that delicious lost morning with it, was a leap into cosmopolitanism that I deeply wanted. Why should I live in a country so narrow-minded that it banned Sunday newspapers? How humiliating, I used to feel, my anger at the United Church and all the complacent covey of bigots—nannies of our morality—who delayed Canada's cultural and spiritual development for so long. Only years later, as a reporter working in "dry" states, forced to go to bootleggers and hide bottles in brown paper bags, did I learn that many parts of the U.S. had nannies, too.

To me at twenty-one, New York was civilization; its bars open all day, dark, cool, and inviting places at all levels of elegance or grime. Ottawa's dreary taverns with their soiled Formica tables, where only beer was sold, inviting depression and drunkenness, shriveled the soul.

New York liquor stores sold spirits with all the verve and competitive pricing of exuberant private enterprise. In Canada you could buy those beverages of the devil only from a liquor commission run by the provincial government, open for limited hours, invested with a dreary air of bureaucratic lethargy. These were small things in the grand scheme of things, but each visit made me angrier about the narrow-mindedness, the cultural poverty of Canada. Each time I took the train back north I felt more trapped, returning to a country that had little apparent interest in books, no professional theater, few concerts, little dance, no established dance or opera companies—a country blanketed by the snow of moral bigotry and political complacency.

Yet, while New York City beckoned me, there was one aspect of America that I greeted with astonishment, as did many Canadians: Senator Joseph McCarthy.

I was still going to college and was a weekend writer for radio station CFRA. I had no journalism credentials, I was an English major, but the news director let me write and broadcast an inter-pretive roundup of the week's news. Looking at McCarthy's ex-cesses from the outside, I thought, What's so great about the First Amendment, or all that stuff Americans keep going on about, if someone like McCarthy can use it to make a mockery of press freedom, something we couldn't imagine happening in Canada?

My commercial radio weekends led to the CBC and secure employment as a staff announcer on radio and soon television. For half a year I had my own television program, a weekly half hour for children broadcast from the National Museum: easy les-sons in anthropology and natural history.

As I worked on my degree and for the CBC, the conviction mounted that everything that I wanted was happening outside Canada, and now *outside* came to mean Europe, primarily En-gland. While I had found New York beguiling, close friends who had recently gone to London were urging me to join them. Then I became engaged to a lovely young woman, Rosemarie Copland, and we decided we would live in London.

My reading was still heavily weighted toward British au-thors—Orwell, Huxley, Woolf, Lawrence, Joyce, and Waugh. While I started writing a novel and toyed with short stories, my ambition refocused on the theater. I determined to be a play-wright and my theatrical mecca became London, not Broadway.

Rosemarie's father, a noted Australian economist serving as high commissioner to Canada, was dubious about a prospective son-in-law who had so vague a future and argued with me that it was pointless to begin life now in England. Charming, but a place of the past, he said: Australia and Canada were the countries of opportunity, countries of the future. But why, I argued back, begin life in places that have no culture, when in England one would begin at the pinnacle of all the received traditions? Why live in a wilderness, where everything had to start with the crudest beginnings? I was tired of being told that Canada's history lay before it—as the comedians say, it still does. Fine, I said, if one's object was just to make money, but I was not interested in business. I had no friends in business; the commerce students seemed to me and my friends to personify the grayness of that life. Money was the last thing that interested me—then. I wanted, vain young fellow, to create, to make a mark on the world and make it where it was really difficult, not make it easily in this small pond.

And I felt simple wanderlust, hunger for the great places of the world—the places where lives became literature; the cities that carried the glorious patina of having been lived in and written about by Dickens or Waugh or Remarque or Koestler. Who in hell had written about Ottawa or Halifax? Strangely, considering the size of my ambition, it never occurred to me to *be* the one who would fill the void. Hugh MacLennan, the Canadian writer who had struggled against foreign and Canadian indifference, observed in a remark that became famous, "Boy meets girl in Winnipeg, and who cares!" I did not care, and it took me many years to realize my mistake. Boys and girls are interesting anywhere if a writer can make them so, as so many Canadian writers have since done.

Those who felt as I did were not different in their aspirations from young people in Akron, bursting to get to New York, or in Nottingham, dying for London. The difference was that in Canada's case, the whole country felt provincial, a way station, not the final destination.

5

VENERATING STONES

*M*y feelings on arriving in England in June 1955 were like those of a young acolyte to Rome, sure that his faith would soar to new heights with proximity to the fountainhead of its mysteries. And I was not disappointed. How could I be when I had been preparing for this homecoming since my mother first complained about Canadian marmalade?

I was more than literary pilgrim, coming to venerate the stones of my gods, although I venerated every stone in sight. I was very consciously a refugee, granted cultural asylum from Canada. And I was not going back. I had a recurring nightmare in which, for some imposture or other, I was being forced to go back to Canada. In one dream I was actually clinging to iron railings symbolic of London houses, as someone tried to pry my fingers off and put me on a ship.

I delighted in the smallest housekeeping details in setting up my Earls Court bedsit (one-room apartment): shillings for the gas meter, pennies for the hot water geyser; dealing with the iron-monger for a tin opener, the fruiterer, the greengrocer, the baker, the butcher, the fishmonger; entranced by the mundane details of living. Even the different smells in making a cup of tea (gas different, tea different, milk different) became an existential experience. It was a pleasure to go into the steamy ABC tea shop in Earls Court Road, to be served a pot of tea and pieces of toast slathered with butter by a blowzy woman, hair escaping from a funny cap, who called me *Luv*.

Henry Miller, hugely admired by me in those days, observed in *The Air Conditioned Nightmare* that Americans had forgotten how to make bread. The disease had spread to Canada. Would I leave my homeland for a better bread? Yes! As I ate the best toast ever, made from bread heavy and moist enough not to turn to dry cardboard or soggy tissue in the toaster. Is a country civilized, I wondered, which had allowed so basic and pleasant a necessity to be stolen by huge commercial empires that baked a worthless airy substance, however full of supposed vitamins? No, and went on with my list. Canada still made sharp cheddar cheese and smelly Oka, but the national taste was being homogenized by Kraft's bland imperialism. In Britain, on your thick doorstep of bread, you could put Cheshire, or Double Gloucester, or Wensleydale, or Stilton, or a hundred re-gional cheeses as varied as those of France or Italy. In a pub you could wash it down with a draft beer that was not yet corrupted by the American drive to reduce beer to a pale, weak, sweet, gassy imi-tation of noble pilsner and market it with ridiculous macho im-agery. In others words, the fundamentals of life in Britain then had real flavor and pungency after bland, antiseptic Canada.

Some of the fundamentals had more pungency than a fastidious North American might have wished. The slatternly old dear who buttered the toast in the ABC probably did not bathe very often; many did not, as you were aware on the buses and the underground. London was still grimy in those days before the Clean Air Act, with everyone burning coal in their grates. In winter you had to wash your windows once a week to be able to see out and let in a little light. The lavatories in pubs and restaurants were foul-smelling, like the fug in an early-morning tube, or the upper deck of a bus on a rainy day, the air blue with the particular odor of the cheapest cigarettes—Woodbines and Will's Whiffs.

I excused all this. It was part of the flavor of London where you also smelled, and could buy, if you wanted to splurge, Passing Clouds, the most expensive Virginia cigarettes, or the best pipe tobacco.

I kept drawing comparative conclusions from small things. The availability of public lavatories everywhere in London was evidence of a civilized and compassionate society. In Ottawa your bladder could burst for want of a public convenience. One freezing night there, a beer-loaded friend (Peter Hopwood) and I were forced to relieve ourselves against a building. For the rest of the winter two yellow icicles accused us.

The Londoners' love of flowers and their display in every possible window box and garden, in hanging baskets on lampposts and in street flower-sellers' stalls, argued something sound in the British character. The wit and panache of the graphic advertising, quite a revelation to me, showed how stodgy and prosaic the Canadian equivalent was. The perfectly designed London taxi, with rigorously trained driver; the cleanliness and efficiency of buses and tubes and their subsidized low fares; the maintenance of streets and parks, were evidence of a civic culture that balanced the public need with proper investment in infrastructure.

London was a city that worked then, even as it still faced colossal damage from the German bombing. There were gaping bomb sites everywhere, like teeth missing in a face; adjoining walls showing the wallpaper and paint of each sheared-off room, floor above floor; the building shells shored up with thick timbers.

Britain's was still a low wage/low price economy that could afford to keep postmen making two deliveries a day, coal deliverymen humping hundredweight bags of anthracite, Cockney bus clippies (fare-takers), before the Jamaican and Pakistani migrations, earning seven pounds a week. Beer was fifteen pence a pint, three shillings bought a cheap seat in the theater. A thousand pounds a year was considered a comfortable salary, and I had come with about seven hundred in savings from my work at the CBC. I could live on five pounds a week, go to the theater often, explore London, and settle down to write the plays that were going to bring me fame and fortune. I was in paradise. London had everything I wanted: countless bookshops, museums, and galleries; witty, thoughtful, as well as smutty Sunday newspapers; BBC radio for all tastes; prom concerts at the Albert Hall; an endless variety of pubs where frosty regulars soon thawed to newcomers. Their opening hours were bizarre but learnable, and I even grew fond of pub food—Scotch eggs, veal-and-ham pie, pork pies, pickled onions, steak and kidney pie, sausages and mash.

I thought I would never leave. Like millions before me, I agreed with Samuel Johnson, whose haunts I haunted, "If a man is tired of London, he is tired of life."

It was my hobby to explore inner London minutely, street by street, as far east as Whitechapel and west to Hammersmith and

Fulham, and from that first year of exploring on foot I still know it more extensively than any other large city.

I had a cluster of Canadian friends, most like me content to be exiles. Some of them found it hard to make a decent living in London and drifted back. Others have never returned. Some quickly became so English it would take a Henry Higgins to unmask them; others kept their Canadian accents, modified unconsciously like mine by the different rhythms of English speech and by the idiom you inevitably acquired from the English people you worked with. A Canadian, like an American, had the priceless advantage of being unplaceable by his speech in the infinite gradations of the British class structure. As Shaw said, "It is impossible for an Englishman to open his mouth without making some other Englishman despise him." It was much harder to despise a Canadian. Some might condescend, and did, condescension being the art form in human manners the English have perfected above all others. Some might mistake us: the shopkeeper asking sniffily, "Oh, are you an American, then?" But the effect of North American class anonymity had—still has—a magic, soothing effect on the British working classes. They did not at once turn on the derision or mock servility they love to use on their English betters. The first time the coal man in Chelsea called me *Guv'nor* sardonically before he heard me speak, I knew the difference.

Also I knew immediately that I was not English and did not want to try to become English. The young man who had pined to be in England, the boy who had felt vaguely cheated because life had dealt him the wrong national identity, did not want to lose that identity in Britain. Indeed, I was privately a little disturbed when I heard an actress friend mimicking the English to perfection. She was apologetic but said it was necessary in the theater.

There weren't enough parts for Canadian or American voices. But actors are different and, although I had had a taste of it, I did not wish to play a part in real life.

Moreover, which part would I have played? There was not *an* Englishman type, but thousands with different class and regional accents and idioms, ways of dressing and amusing themselves. I had, in fact, played some of them crudely in my own acting days, but confronting the real thing, the living models in all their variety, caused a tiny switch to click; as the English said, "The penny dropped," and I knew I was not an Englishman.

I didn't walk around with a Canadian badge in my lapel, but I was content to be known as "the Canadian." I had settled into my skin as an expatriate, a situation in which it was curiously easier to *feel* Canadian.

In the plays I was writing, however, I unconsciously appropriated stock English characters, a serious mistake. I knew few English people firsthand then, so I was filching from literary models. I had some encouragement from an agent, but playwriting was obviously not going to mean immediate security. When Rosemarie's parents reluctantly consented to our marriage after she finished her degree in Canada, I had a year in which to establish myself in something gainful. As my first autumn in London advanced, so did my anxiety. I bombarded the BBC and the newly founded Independent Television with applications. Independent Television News, then just opening, hired me temporarily as a newswriter for nine pounds a week. The job lasted three months, taught me how little I knew about journalism, and got me an introduction to Reuters News Agency. That intimidating place— noisy, glamorous, demanding—gave me a six-week trial and then hired me permanently as a subeditor.

The work was difficult at first, learning to pound out crisp wire-service prose with no wasted words and no ambiguities, yet including all necessary facts, all checked and accurate, put in the right order, if possible with some grace and rhythm. And do it in no time. Painfully I learned and began to advance up the Central Desk, quite pleased that I had a niche with British colleagues who respected me. To work in fabled Fleet Street was an abiding pleasure; to learn all the small bits of its micro-ecosystem, the hidden pubs in the narrow lanes, the place where you could get tomorrow's papers tonight, the little cafés where I got my sandwiches made for the all-night shift; the tea trolley with its custard tarts, the "tea boys," middle-aged male messengers constantly on patrol with large enamel pitchers of hot milky tea; the tobacconists at the Temple Bar who sold the Proctor's Mixture (Virginia, Havana leaf, and Latakia) I smoked; the rushing newspaper vans, the offices of the provincial newspapers I began to know from the proofs of editorials they rushed over to Reuters to be "milked" for overseas newspapers.

After two months in my bedsit I ran into Jim Miller, whom I knew slightly from Carleton. We agreed to find a flat we could share until Rosemarie and I got married. We found one in Redcliffe Gardens and banished some of the London beige by repainting it ourselves. Then a couple, Ken and Marilyn Wells, moved in, and it gradually became a transit camp for various itinerants. That meant nonstop bull sessions by Canadians alternately disgruntled and enchanted with Britain, deconstructing political articles in the *Spectator* and *Statesman*, every play review by Kenneth Tynan. For refreshment we would creep to the corner pub, feeling our way by hands on railings and walls through the last of the London "pea soupers," which ended when it became illegal to burn unprocessed coal. All fun but no time for my writing. So I pulled out to find a bedsitter a few streets away in Courtfield Gardens. I still measured my independence by my ability to move all my possessions, dirty milk bottles included, in one London taxi.

The shift work at Reuters gave me little blocks of time (five days off after nine days on the all-night shift), more precious because so hard-earned, and I began to take little forays into the English countryside. I would choose a place, take the train there, and walk for several days to a town from which I could catch another train back to London. The experience brought to the surface another emotion that had been latent in my feelings about Canada, a different sense of freedom.

I could set out to walk across country, following a good map, from village to village, through country tilled and shaped by man's hand for perhaps two thousand years. Not the noble but often virgin landscape of Canada, where a belt of spruce might run for a hundred miles, dark and impenetrable; where you might still tread where no human had ever trodden. Here in Surrey or Hampshire, you walked where countless men had walked and where their ghosts still walked. If you found a stretch of uncut woodland, it lasted a few hundred yards instead of miles. Every few miles, nestled into its hollow or fold was a village, each with its Norman or Saxon church to visit, each with pubs for refreshment and conversation. I might decide one morning to cover fifteen miles that day and find a bed five villages away but, if I got tired or diverted by something, I could change my ambition or direction anytime. Land that has been lived in for so long has a network of footpaths and small lanes, worn by local convenience over the centuries and preserved as rights of way by English common law. If the topographical survey maps showed a dotted line across someone's field, through his farmyard, or by his Elizabethan manor house, you had the right to walk it. As long as you closed the gates, used the stiles, and respected his crops and livestock, you could walk all over England on private property where ancient rights had been established.

I loved that and loved the land. I have several paintings by a Suffolk artist, Hugh Boycott Brown. One shows a country road through hedgerows leading to the small village of Iken, its houses settled into their hollow like birds in a nest, only half visible. In the distance is the sea. It is early spring, recognizable by the cast of light and the color of the English sky, so evocative that I feel I can smell the newly turned soil in the fields or see the wild primroses around the bend.

Those were the first of many walking trips in England and France, some more ambitious, but they gave me the sweetest pleasure.

In London, I ate in glum eateries, square shop spaces that appeared to have been decorated, furnished, and staffed in the 1920s and never altered. A graying lace curtain covered the lower half of the window; the walls were serviceable cream enamel above the green wainscoting; the tables and chairs wore dark varnish; the tablecloths were unfresh and the cutlery huge, forks and spoons left from Victorian and Edwardian dinners, when the British gorged themselves to keep out the cold. With these giant implements, now tarnished, the electroplating scuffed off to dull metal, the imitation bone knife handles yellowed and chipped, you would eat brown Windsor soup that tasted like Bovril (a meat extract) and flour cooked together, and razor-thin slices of indeterminate meat, dark gray except for an iridescent sheen, like gasoline puddles, presumably marks of extreme age. You finished with some doughy flan or tinned fruit swimming in prefabricated custard. If you insisted on coffee, it was a black liquid almost all chicory, which brown sugar converted to a passable syrup and milk made a dirty gray, like water that socks have been washed in. I sat there, hiding behind the *New Statesman* or staring at the rain falling on the Fulham Road or Kensington High Street. That penance cost something like four shillings and sixpence. I was no gourmet and had little restaurant experience. If this was English food, so be it.

But it was not real English food. That I found in the small hotels, the little inns, the pubs I encountered on my country walks: enormous breakfasts with the cost of the lodging, porridge, eggs, bacon, sausage, grilled tomato or kipper and tomato, and all the toast, tea, and marmalade I could consume. A plowman's lunch in a pub, slabs of the local cheese and bread, Branston pickle, or a slice of veal-and-ham pie and a pint of bitter. In the evening, homemade steak, kidney, and mushroom pie or a mixed grill of lamb chop, kidney, ham, mushroom, and tomato; desserts of rich trifle, for the same price as the gray fare in the city.

I carried a haversack with a small change of clothing and a raincoat, some paperback books, and an ash stick. I still have it fifty years later, but the bend in the crook is gradually straightening itself out.

On the train to Victoria Station, arriving in London in the late spring sunset, walking home to Courtfield Gardens off Cromwell Road, with each return London belonged more legitimately to me; I had better credentials to be there because I carried the tan of Sussex sun on my face and the dust of England on my shoes.

Nowhere in Canada could offer the absence of blackflies, of mosquitoes, or serious snakes or poison ivy, of which England was blessedly free; or the singing of larks, blackbirds, thrushes, and occasional cuckoos in the woods and hedgerows; nor could Canada offer the feast of beautiful village gardens, in grand houses or humble, the unbelievable profusion of spring flowers set against old stone or old brick; lawns green in February and mown like putting greens. No place in Canada offered churches a thousand years old, mossy with history. To have this was worth London bathwater so hard it barely lathered the soap, toilet paper then so aggressively waterproof that I once typed a letter on several sheets.

. . .

In 1956, Nikita Khrushchev's speech attacking Stalin at the Twentieth Party Congress offered the first glimmer of change in Moscow's rigid totalitarianism, as his use of Soviet tanks to crush the Hungarian uprising that fall snuffed it out. Both stories shook the world, and some segments of them passed through my battered upright Royal typewriter on the Reuters Central Desk. But the story that distracted attention, indeed, some felt, provided Khrushchev with a cloak for his brutality in Budapest, was the Suez crisis.

It was also the event that caused my political awakening, the first political happening to engage my private emotions. It brought my first taste of disillusionment with the British.

Egypt's feisty president, Gamal Abdel Nasser, had led the revolution that deposed the corrupt King Farouk. Nasser dreamed of reawakening pan-Arab solidarity to restore the might that had once challenged European civilization. But Nasser had few resources beyond the wild rhetoric of Cairo Radio—and the Suez Canal, the piece of Victorian engineering that cut thousands of miles from the voyage around Africa to Asia.

Nasser wanted a high dam at Aswan to tame the immemorial

flooding of the Nile and thus irrigate its arable land. The Soviets offered to build it; alarmed, the United States offered a better deal and Nasser accepted. But John Foster Dulles, President Eisenhower's secretary of state, changed his mind abruptly and withdrew the offer. Nasser promptly nationalized the canal.

The canal was owned by an Anglo-French consortium. Its closure was unthinkable to two nations that had seats on the UN Security Council and which still nursed imperial illusions. France had only just been forced out of Vietnam, but not yet out of Algeria. The winds of change that would convert most of Britain's African empire to independence had only begun to whisper of impotence and the need for a new role at home.

In Britain and France there was outrage and an immediate growl from the atavistic forces that had traditionally solved such affronts by sending in the gunboats.

That September, Rosemarie and I were married at St. Columba's in Pont Street, her parents swallowing their reluctance and giving us an elegant lunch at the Hyde Park Hotel.

We spent the first week of our honeymoon at Stratford-on-Avon, where we could see stars such as Peggy Ashcroft and Alan Badel in a different Shakespeare each night. In the days we bicycled and walked about the Shakespeare country. The second week we sailed off the south coast in a boat chartered cheaply from an old fellow I'd met on a walk near Chichester. She was a forty-four-foot Dutch centerboard cruiser built before World War I, beautiful to behold but heavy and old-fashioned in her gear. We sailed her through some close shaves with the tides and fogs of the Solent and the languid estuaries of the Isle of Wight. Each piece of coast was resonant with significance from the reading of my youth, and the special mystique, however grim the physical conditions, of messing about in boats.

I didn't believe for a moment that Prime Minister Anthony Eden would use force against Nasser. Nor did Dulles, apparently, but he reckoned without the Israelis. In secret collusion with Britain and France, Israel attacked Egypt across the Sinai Peninsula, creating the pretext for Anglo-French military action, ostensibly to protect canal traffic.

Now all of England was on fire. As the crisis mounted, we came back to London and settled temporarily for a large bedsit in Courtfield Gardens.

In that room we heard the stunning news that the British were bombing Port Said and landing paratroopers. The radio was on the Victorian mantelpiece and I stood by it, incredulous. I could not understand how the reasonable and civilized Brits—so recently bombed themselves—could justify bombing Egyptian civilians. My reaction was naive, my faith in some abstract British reasonableness blinding me. Eden, who had earned great moral credit for resigning in protest over Chamberlain's appeasement of Hitler, grossly misapplied the analogy to Nasser. Resistance to, not appeasement of, dictators provided a music still thrilling to some of the British public but ignored the realities of Britain's economic decline. (Margaret Thatcher played the same tunes in the Falklands and saw her popularity soar, but she had the cooperation of the United States, as Eden did not.) The Eisenhower administration called on the British, French, and Israelis to stop hostilities and voted against its wartime allies in the United Nations. Eden retired, humiliated and ill. It was Canada's creative diplomacy that came up not only with a solution but a model for United Nations action, the UN peacekeeping force. For this, Lester Pearson, Canada's external affairs minister, won the Nobel Peace Prize and went on to become prime minister.

I had a front-row seat as the crisis convulsed the British press:

part of my job at Reuters was selecting and summarizing the violently opposed opinions of British editors for transmission around the world. What particularly inspired me was the behavior of the BBC. To the fury of the Tory government, the BBC faithfully reflected in its home news and world service the divisions in the country. Heaped with abuse by Conservatives in Parliament, who demanded that the BBC reflect government policy, the BBC replied that it would protect the reputation it had established in World War II. It was a stunning display of integrity for public broadcasters, whose independence is always nuanced.

Finally, Suez made me realize that, as former colonial subjects, Canadians had some useful understanding of the new forces in the world. They were in tune with the often exasperating but fully justified aspirations of British and French colonies that wanted sovereignty and independence.

Ironically, Canadians soon found themselves struggling against a new imperial power. Some nationalists claimed that Canada had ceased to be a colony of Britain only to become one of the United States. But that was in the future. In 1956, U.S. doctrines firmly supported independence for the former colonies of the British and French empires: Americans did so from principles made imperative by their own history but doubly imperative because decolonization was becoming a major psychological battleground in the Cold War. The Soviets under Khrushchev tried at every turn to outreach and outbid the West in welcoming emerging nations to the socialist camp.

That exercise received a setback in the other major event of 1956, the uprising against Soviet rule in Hungary and its brutal suppression by Moscow. That was a little hard to explain to "freedom-loving peoples everywhere," a favorite Soviet phrase, but it was more easily fudged because they also had Suez to scream about. The world's two leading old imperial powers, Britain and France, however dog-eared now, attacking a developing country and former suzerainty like Egypt, touched a frenzied chord in the Third World, which viewed the Hungarian episode with relative indifference.

The last terse appeals by the Hungarian Freedom Fighters, about to be wiped out by Soviet troops, came in broken phrases through radio monitors in Austria and England, and through our wires in Fleet Street. It was a moment of deep pathos, underscoring the unreal expectations they had nourished from taking the encouragement of Radio Free Europe and the Voice of America too literally. They thought it meant active backing, that the mighty American president who had liberated Europe from Hitler would stop Moscow from crushing them. It was not so: the messianic rhetoric of John Foster Dulles, who made the struggle sound like a holy war against the Antichrist, did not mean that the prudent soldier Eisenhower would risk World War III. The spheres of influence between East and West were tacitly recognized: Hungary was Moscow's to control.

That year gave me an early perspective on the Cold War I was to cover for so much of my career, a little to one side and accustomed to skepticism of American behavior. Canadian diplomats in Cold War listening posts were a useful resource: they had good information and did not have to bend their reporting to current Washington ideology. One example was Finland: Washington saw the Finns as being dangerously cozy with Moscow. Ottawa saw them skillfully keeping the Soviets at arm's length, a view my own reporting confirmed. British diplomats also viewed the Cold War with un-American detachment, and not without a certain pleasure in seeing both Moscow and Washington discomfited.

As the Cold War advanced—and I found myself fortuitously

present at some of the most dramatic moments—that Canadian skepticism of Washington, that ironic distance heightened by the needling cynicism of British briefings, further nourished by British left-wing views I found congenial, informed me, personally and professionally. The effort to be uncommitted (such a Canadian emotion!) probably led me sometimes to press my skepticism of American motives too far, but it usually sprang back.

Of course, such heavy politics occupied us very little, in our middle twenties, newlyweds, entranced with the adult freedoms that, in a time when to live together you got married, we associated with the freedom of London itself. We found a small basement flat in Glebe Place in Chelsea, and my theatrical ambitions soared each day as I passed the Royal Court Theatre in Sloane Square by the underground station that led to Fleet Street. It was at that moment the birthplace of an exciting renaissance in the British theater, ignited by the production of John Osborne's *Look Back in Anger*—a play similar in theme to one I had written in Ottawa, but mine was provincial and unsophisticated compared to Osborne's. My agent had sent the Royal Court a new play of mine, and I lived a daily agony of hope and gloom until they rejected it.

I could not mourn for long, however, because Rosemarie was pregnant, and we felt obliged to find a bigger flat. The search produced one that had plenty of space, but it was in a dreary suburb, Bounds Green, miles away in North London. If I could undo that move, I would. We exchanged the charm and sophistication of Chelsea—with easy access to everything pleasant in London—for a soulless street of two-story brick double-terrace houses, two front doors, one flat downstairs, one up, each with a strip of garden and a coal bin at the back. It was respectable, with lace curtains in every window, its neat parade of small shops down the road, its matched laburnum trees all dripping yellow blossoms on schedule.

There was a coal grate in each room, the one in the dining room off the kitchen also created hot water, or was supposed to. Each morning I lit a new coal fire, hauling coal from the bin at the bottom of the garden. The flat was spacious, furnished, affordable; when you were inside with the fire going, the *Third Program* on the radio, and a good book from the lending library, or with friends sitting over a bottle of seven-shilling wine, it was snug and homey. But the streets we negotiated—I to the Northern Line tube station, Rosemarie for the daily shopping in the English style— were barren and dispiriting.

. . .

In the meantime, Dad, now fifty, in his last gesture to adventure and travel, had astonished us all by chucking his career with the RCMP and moving my mother and younger brother Michael to London to become an attaché at Canada House.

"He was like a boy when he got here," my mother said. "Put us in the hotel and went off walking all over London. God knows what he got up to!"

He had given up the rank of superintendent and position as commandant of the RCMP Training Division in Rockcliffe, with all the dignities and perks the service offers its most senior officers, plus a ceremonial role as an aide-de-camp to the governor-general, to take a relatively junior job in External Affairs. While Canada's foreign service had a social cachet the RCMP did not, it was a daring move for him. He'd had one serious heart attack, and bypass operations had yet to arrive. He suffered from angina and took nitroglycerine pills, and was supposed to watch his food, drink, and smoking—but didn't. In addition to the stress of changing careers, he traveled constantly around Europe to oversee security arrangements in Canadian embassies.

Dad had the personal style to carry it off, as though he had been appointed high commissioner himself, and came to London determined to enjoy it. My mother was both terrified of the responsibility and "thrilled to bits," as she said, to be actually living in the country she had extolled as the antechamber to heaven. My brother Hugh, four years younger, also just married, was now a newly minted sublieutenant in the Canadian navy based at Greenwich. So the whole family was united that Christmas in London.

Friends gave us their large English pram and I had the pleasure of walking it empty one evening the entire length of Bayswater between Notting Hill Gate and Marble Arch, in those days thick with prostitutes. Their remarks as I bowled along with the bouncing pram were choice: "Wages of sin, luv?" or, "My friend'll mind the baby if you want to come in for a good time."

I was so sure that we would stay in England permanently that when our daughter Cathy was born in July 1957, we did not register her as a Canadian.

We settled with the baby in the flat at Bounds Green and into the life we could afford on eighteen pounds a week plus overtime. We washed the cloth nappies (diapers) by hand, hung them in the coal-smoky air on the garden clothesline, sometimes had to run into the street in our nightclothes to get change in shillings from the milkman for the electricity meter. We learned how quickly five hundred weight of coal disappeared by forgetting to order, forcing me to fish with a flashlight through a mound of coal dust for the few burnable lumps. For entertainment, we read (that was my year for Dostoyevsky), played our few LPs, and listened to the BBC.

In the cold front room (it was too much trouble to light another fire) I tried writing short stories instead of plays, and a novel with the silly but revealing title *Diary of an UnCanadian*, about, amazingly, a young Canadian who has intellectual pretensions, who yearns to be a writer, who leaves Canada—coincidentally on the same ship I had—then gets bogged down in the enervating charms of London.

My writing was neglected when I felt I had to make more money. CBC News in Toronto needed freelancers to do radio news pieces from London, and I fell into the pattern of regular moonlighting. Every morning I would get up at six and go down the street for an armful of the ten London dailies and study them for an hour. At 7 A.M., with several offerings in mind, I would call the CBC producer, trying to ring before the other freelancers tied up his line. If he bought one or more stories, I would write them quickly and go to the studios in the old Langham Hotel across Portland Place from Broadcasting House.

After broadcasting my pieces to Canada, I would go down to Fleet Street to begin my shift at Reuters. Each CBC story paid seven or ten pounds, and with only three a week I could more than double my Reuters salary. Since at Reuters I edited and rewrote mostly world news, and London was still the big Cold War listening post and diplomatic intelligence center, there was no shortage of information. I developed a knack for producing think pieces that leaned heavily on "diplomatic sources . . . British officials . . . Western circles."

The CBC thus gave me a different level of skills, as a broadcast journalist.

With comic deliberation and trepidation, given my blighted affair with the old Jaguar, we bought a 1934 Austin 7 for twenty-five pounds, about sixty-seven dollars—coincidentally the price of parting with the Jag. The Austin was one of those little black boxes that always ran. It had a starting handle (crank) permanently sticking through the front bumper—no electric starter—and once I had learned how to crank it with my thumb on the correct side, it always started and seemed an amazing advance in our standard of living.

It carried the heavy weekly shopping, took us on little trips to the country, and putt-putted up to the grand portals of my parents' apartment building, whose doorman wanted to hide it from the Bentleys and Rovers he considered suitable embellishments for his doorway.

Englishmen love talking cars, and in the lulls between stories on the Central Desk, heavy automotive wisdom was passed over the tea mugs and tobacco smoke. I felt even more intimate with those who had a rickety car to talk about instead of babies and 2 A.M. feedings.

My growing earnings and Rosemarie's second pregnancy convinced us to live somewhere more cheerful. We found a tiny but charming Georgian cottage in Highgate and bought a five-year lease. We furnished it from Harrods auctions for a hundred pounds. It didn't take much, our doll's house, but with three bedrooms, living room, dining room and kitchen, and a small garden, it was a big step in sophistication. We put Daisy Oxner's silver candelabra on our small mahogany table, had friends to dinner, and felt we had come a long way in the world.

Highgate is fashionable and charming, an eighteenth-century village on a steep hill north of Hampstead. Karl Marx is buried in Highgate's moody cemetery and his plinth was a shrine for visiting communists. The Georgian facades were graceful. The Flask, a pub at the top of the hill, had a shady garden for summer drinks where cherry blossoms floated into your beer, and it was a comfortable walk with small children to Kenwood and Hampstead Heath.

Highgate village also provided an excellent young doctor, Chris Hindley, who to my admiration had refused lucrative offers to emigrate to practice in Canada or the U.S. because he believed in the British National Health Service. He and the excellent local authority baby clinic provided admirable pre- and postnatal attention when our son Ian appeared in February 1959.

I now had two children with British birth certificates, and it never occurred to me to do anything but recognize their consequent British citizenship. I don't remember any discussion. Rosemarie had a British passport as she had been born in London, and my Canadian citizenship gave me full rights in Britain.

Canadian politics had held no interest for me in the era of prime ministers Mackenzie King and Louis St. Laurent, aptly described by the Toronto writer Jack McLeod as decades "of sonorous mush," and I have never lived there to vote since then.

My distaste got further nourishment when Prime Minister John Diefenbaker came to London. Freelancing for the CBC, I heard him address the Empire League, probably the most reactionary bunch of unreconstructed imperialists as ever slapped a native or sipped pink gin in Delhi. Diefenbaker delivered an old-fashioned imperialist harangue that was embarrassing to listen to. In London he sounded totally out of tune with the times, and most British papers ignored him.

Then I had to interview him. He submitted to my questions somewhat grouchily after breakfast in his Park Lane hotel suite. In the lobby I checked the recorder and found that the tape was blank. Tape recorders work about as reliably for me as outboard motors. I debated telling the CBC there was something wrong with the machine, but the need for future assignments drove me back upstairs. After I explained to an aide, terrible sounds came from the other room, but, unable to pass up a CBC interview, a very angry prime minister reemerged and reanswered the same questions.

One of my frequent tasks at Reuters was to edit President Eisenhower's news conferences. Since I was the North American on the Central Desk, they thought I could make coherent stories from Ike's famously opaque language—another excuse for the running sarcasm in that newsroom for most things American. If many of those journalists had had a chance to emigrate to the States out of the pinched living in Britain, they might have jumped. Sublimated envy was one source of the gentle anti-Americanism that seemed part of the climate in England then: loyalty in the fundamentals like competition in space or the Cold War, but reflexive distaste for the culture that was beginning to encroach on Britain's own. One interesting phenomenon in the television age is elitist scorn for the culture that produces programs your own people can't resist. I got some corrective each Sunday evening from Alistair Cooke's radio show *Letter from America*; it treated American foibles in a tart but affectionate essay and was hugely popular in England. But the journalistic air I breathed in Fleet Street was heavy with booze fumes, tobacco, and putdowns of America. Londoners might cheer Eisenhower when he visited in 1959 to boost Harold Macmillan in a general election, but the tabloids they read reduced America to a saucy caricature. Not that America didn't provide ammunition.

When Ike's postmaster general, Arthur Summerfield, banned *Lady Chatterley's Lover* from the U.S. mails as "an obscene and filthy work," the hilarity in Britain made it seem infinitely more worldly, civilized, and grown-up. I knew the British had banned *Lady Chatterley* themselves thirty years earlier, but not now, not in 1959!

In November that year, my father died suddenly in Athens. He had suffered a second heart attack the previous year in Paris and had gradually recovered. This third attack was fatal. The Canadian government brought his body back to London and there he was cremated. He was only fifty-three. My mother and Michael moved back to Ottawa.

I had begun looking for an opportunity beyond Reuters. The discipline and standards they exacted were superb. For journalists it was the equivalent of basic training in a British Guards regiment: spartan, ill paid, and elite. I had burrowed into British life intimately enough to be elected an officer in the Reuters chapter of the National Union of Journalists. I had advanced regularly up the desk, been given more responsibility, like copytaster (filing editor) and occasionally editor-in-charge, and they had rewarded me with a colorful assignment as a correspondent for two weeks in Tangier, but I thought I could face years ahead on the Central Desk.

So I was quite receptive to the first British offer that came along, from the *Financial Times*, wages 50 percent more than my Reuters salary, and I agreed to move after the first of the year.

Then I got a call from NBC. Their second London correspondent, John Chancellor, wanted a weekend off, and through the CBC they had heard of me. I covered for him, broadcast several radio stories to New York, and got hired full-time.

So overnight I became an American broadcaster, quite casually transferring my fate from a most British institution to a very American one in the decade that so traumatized and transformed America and, as it turned out, vastly changed my life.

Culturally at first the change was superficial. We continued living in a style Americans considered mean: our small cottage, its kitchen and bathroom primitive by American standards; shopping in the small-scale English way.

NBC bureau chief Joseph C. Harsch had hired me as an editorial assistant and backup reporter. But when Chancellor was transferred to Moscow, they made me a correspondent in his place. Because British news was our principal commodity, I became immersed in British affairs even more than while at Reuters. I now began to go regularly to the House of Commons and off-the-record briefings at the Foreign Office and 10 Downing Street along with American journalistic stars like Flora Lewis, Drew Middleton, and Eric Sevareid. To hear their sharp, skeptical questions and the subtle spinning of the British officials took my education to another level. Still another was learning to feed the insatiable American market for stories of British quaintness and eccentricity.

Rosemarie and I had ignored television until then, but we now got our first set, which had the effect of immersing me still more deeply in British culture. When David Frost & Company began the satirical *That Was the Week that Was*, it became essential viewing on Saturday nights. You stayed home: it was too delicious, unthinkable to miss. So, my culture, politically and socially, became even more British. I was working for Americans but getting almost no American acculturation.

New York soon began using me as a fireman correspondent. In the first few months with NBC, I spent five weeks in the Congo, four in France, and two in Berlin. I had been so much away from my family that NBC allowed me to take Rosemarie and the two small children to Berlin.

This was in late October 1960, and one assignment was to do

advance pieces on Berliners' reactions to either a Kennedy or a Nixon victory. We were staying in the new Berlin Hilton, which stood almost alone in a bombed-out wasteland, a taunting symbol of Western prosperity to communist East Berlin. The U.S. Information Service mounted a screening of the first Kennedy-Nixon TV debate. The Hilton ballroom was jammed with influential Berliners who, like Republicans at home, expected Nixon, the accomplished debater, to demolish the callow young Senator Kennedy. The Berliners emerged deeply depressed by what they saw. Nixon, Eisenhower's reliably anticommunist vice president, had been a known quantity; Kennedy was cause for anxiety.

Back in London, my early TV experience in Canada came into play. Joe Harsch continued writing three columns a week for the *Christian Science Monitor* and preferred the simplicity of radio for his broadcasting. So New York's demand for television pieces from the bureau increasingly fell to me. Producers for *The Huntley-Brinkley Report* began coming to London to work with me while other NBC programs asked for pieces I could produce myself.

One mind-opening exercise was a half hour on American influence in Britain, a vogue subject in magazines that season. American methods of mass production and marketing of consumer durables were just beginning to transform British homes, still mostly innocent of refrigerators, washing machines, or dishwashers. The introduction of commercial television and the many imported American programs helped push this consumer revolution.

I found myself as a reporter pondering which had produced the greater impact on the British standard of living: socialist legislation nationalizing health care, coal mines, and railroads, or American-style marketing of modern kitchens and home improvements. I surprised myself by concluding probably the latter, my one reservation being the National Health Service.

A New York producer, George Murray, came to have dinner at home with us. He was a big man and looked too large for our miniature rooms. As I drove him back into central London, he said bluntly, "Why are you living in a dump like that? Isn't NBC paying you enough to afford something better?"

It was more generously meant than it sounds, but it stung. But the problem was no longer money. It was my frequent absence. The NBC job grew more diverting each month. When President and Mrs. Kennedy came to Europe, I followed them to Vienna and Paris. I was sent to Sweden, Portugal, Algeria, Finland, Ireland, Belgium, and France many times, then to New York to give me a tryout as an anchorman on a summer series called *This Is NBC News*. In August 1961, I was sent to Berlin to cover the bureau for a month and happened to arrive the night the East Germans began erecting the Berlin Wall. That kept me there for weeks, sharing with other correspondents the constant flow of stories day and night.

In the first few days, American and East German tanks faced each other at the new checkpoints, and the world wondered whether this would be the spark that ignited nuclear war. In those days I came to admire the cool professionalism of the U.S. Army.

Often at night I patrolled the newly rising wall, parking my rented VW as close as I could get. One rainy night I came upon an outpost in the American sector where a young officer and some troops were guarding the approach to a bridge leading to East Berlin. The wall, cement blocks then about chest high, blocked the middle of the bridge. The soldiers offered me coffee and we chatted until a radio squawked and one of them said, "The general's coming." They roused themselves in an unpanicked way to look alert and a minute later the general and a couple of aides drove up in a jeep. The young officer reported all quiet, but the general wanted a look over the bridge. Accompanied by a sergeant with a flashlight, he walked up the bridge to the wall with me tagging along. No sign of life on the other side. The tall general peered over the wall and the sergeant shone his flashlight down, discovering two East German soldiers slumped together asleep. They must have been exhausted because the flashlight didn't wake them, but a drop of rain fell off the lip of the general's helmet and splashed on the face of one of the sleepers. They sprang up in alarm, grabbing their weapons, but the general laughed and we walked back down the bridge. I liked his relaxed attitude. If a guy like this was in charge, there wouldn't be any panic or itchy trigger fingers.

On a Sunday, a crowd of West Berliners came up to heckle East German masons who were reluctantly and sloppily adding blocks to the wall. As the westerners shouted abuse, an East German loudspeaker truck arrived and began broadcasting slogans, deafening everyone. The westerners vented their rage by hurling small paving stones at the truck, whereupon an armored water cannon began shooting powerful jets of water at them. The West Berliners responded with even more stones. At this point American soldiers moved in with fixed bayonets and began pushing the westerners away from the Wall. Watching this and feeling the rising anger of the West Berliners, I said somewhat heatedly to the captain, "Why are you stopping them?"

He said in the most casual and easy way, "Hell, I'm not going to start World War III so some Germans can throw stones at each other." Again I felt that, at least on the ground, this crisis was in good hands.

I also developed lasting affection for the man who had become my mentor at NBC, Reuven Frank, originator and producer of *The Huntley-Brinkley Report*. It was he who had made me a correspondent. A few days into the crisis I slipped into East Berlin with a German student to feel the mood on the other side of the wall. Before lunch we were arrested and my still camera seized. We were held about twelve hours, quite unnerving when I was questioned repeatedly about why I had been taking pictures, how much the CIA was paying me, and so on. At midnight when we were released and got back to the NBC bureau, I found that Reuven had gone looking for me, from one East Berlin police station to another—using his Yiddish!

Some time after that, NBC suggested that I become an American citizen. Interestingly, I had no resistance to that and arranged to go to the States where, they said, it would be a simple matter to get a congressman to fix it. They made it sound so matter-of-fact, I didn't question it. I went to New York and, with a friendly PR man, Milt Brown, on to Washington, where we called on the network's chief lobbyist.

That gentleman was not pleased. Why was New York bothering him with stuff like this, indicating me, when they knew he had important legislation on hand, a tough sell with congressman so and so? As we left I said to myself, "Well, if that's all my citizenship means to you, to hell with it!" As though the indifference to my citizenship were his problem, not mine. Smarting from the snub I went back to London, and in the constant pressure of exciting events to cover the issue was forgotten.

In two weeks off I wrote another play and submitted it to BBC Television. They rejected it, but my new agent, Margaret Ramsey, thought it was promising. She was becoming a legend in the British theater for nurturing playwrights such as Robert Bolt and wanted to help me develop. I walked on air out of her office, fully resolved to reapply myself to plays. The next day I had to go to Finland on a story and the playwriting went back into cold storage.

Now NBC decided I should move to the U.S. At first I put them off because I was needed at home, and my constant traveling was undermining our marriage. Six months later NBC pressed again and I flew to New York to discuss my future—arriving the night Kennedy announced the discovery of Soviet missiles in Cuba.

For weeks, Republicans had been charging that the Kennedy administration was ignoring just such a threat, and my first assumption was that the crisis was a tactic in the midterm election campaign. But in Washington, where I was sent immediately to help out, my NBC colleagues were taking it with the utmost gravity. In the Pentagon newsroom I overheard a fellow correspondent, Herb Kaplow, asking his wife to load the station wagon with the children, water, and blankets, and drive west.

After two days, NBC suggested I use my Canadian passport to go to Cuba, and I did, flying to Mexico City and buying a ticket to Havana on Cubana Airlines. The plane was empty except for me, a Japanese, and three European reporters. All of us were arrested at Havana airport and confined for nine days in the Capri Hotel, with armed guards outside our rooms. The Japanese newspaperman had a radio, and for days we heard NBC News from Miami saying I was missing. Our phones were blocked at the switchboard, but the Japanese suggested tapping into the conduit of phone lines running up the building. Cutting into many wires, we eventually got a dial tone, called the Reuters office, and gave them our names and nationalities.

There was a funny sequel. A few minutes after we replaced the plate over the phone connection behind my bed, a telephone operator came to speak to the guards. The reporter for *Stern*, who spoke Spanish, heard her say, "Someone has been phoning from the empty room."

We knew there were rooms down the hall sometimes used by Cuban bridal couples favored by the state but which were empty during the crisis. One guard took the elevator down. A few minutes later a squad of soldiers appeared with an officer. In the best Hollywood manner he approached the room she indicated and shouted to the suspect to come out. When no one did, he threw himself theatrically against the door. Finally they produced a key, unlocked it, charged in, and came out empty-handed while we watched innocently from the end of the hall.

Within hours NBC had the story of our confinement, but we had to wait several more days until people from our embassies were allowed to visit and we were released.

I was free for four days, sampling the strangely detached atmosphere in Havana after the crisis had broken. Then, while having dinner with a diplomat, I heard a squeal of brakes, and soldiers with guns ran into the restaurant and hauled me off to a small jail. After three insalubrious days I was deported. At the airport they let me buy a box of Havana cigars, which I gave to NBC's White House correspondent, Sander Vanocur, who gave them to Pierre Salinger, who gave them to President Kennedy.

Twenty-five years later, for *The MacNeil-Lehrer NewsHour*, I did one of the marathon late-night interviews with Fidel Castro. During a break I told him my story from 1962. As he listened he slumped in his chair, curling up into a sort of fetal crouch. But as he said nothing, I couldn't make anything of that. In the interview, though typically long-winded, he was cogent, intellectually spirited, even playful; still the leading actor in the personal cold war he had played so skillfully: repressing his own people while conjuring up for his small nation a psychological importance to bedevil the United States for decades.

In my partly conscious/partly-not running tally of things that drew me to the U.S. or Canada, it amused me that Canada continued to deal with Castro, one of Ottawa's ways of keeping a little distance from Washington. But then Ottawa didn't have thousands of Cuban exiles primed for instant riot at any softening in Washington.

Back in New York, I appeared on *Today* and other NBC shows to talk about my treatment in Havana, both gratified by the attention and embarrassed at the tendency of NBC PR handouts to overdramatize the experience. More within my control was an article for the *New York Times Magazine*.

At the end of 1962, our personal problems had reached a point at which Rosemarie and I arranged to separate for a time. For her own well-being she needed to be relieved of the responsibility of looking after two children. She stayed in London and I moved to Washington for NBC, taking Cathy and Ian, now six and four, with me.

6

A FRESH START

*I*t is certainly part of the American character to move on, make a fresh start, in effect re-create yourself. It appeals to me because it is so demonstrably part of my family's character—and mine.

I felt it strongly arriving in Washington in March 1963. It lifted my spirits to come to this gleaming city, spring already tasteable in the mild air; the city luminous with the infectious youth and verve of a president, now tempered and confident from the two climactic showdowns of the Cold War, Berlin and Cuba.

Assigned at first to the State Department, I attended Kennedy's press conferences in the auditorium there, too new to risk asking questions myself, but there for the experience, pleasure in his performance, his easy grasp of the facts, and his dry wit.

I soon saw a different side of Washington. The NBC bureau chief, Bill Monroe, a crusading broadcaster in his native New Orleans, had commissioned a documentary on the racial situation in the District of Columbia and I became the reporter. Every day at the bus station you could see a trickle of poor blacks swelling the southern migration into D.C. to live in squalor, unemployed, undernourished. In one kitchen I filmed rats brazenly staring down at me through a large hole in the ceiling. All this a few blocks from the White House.

Race became a major assignment that summer. I was sent briefly to Birmingham, Alabama, as civil rights protests grew and white resistance became fiercer, but my own patch of the civil rights story was in Cambridge, Maryland. That stretch of the Eastern Shore would have joined the Confederacy if Lincoln hadn't marched troops around the top of Chesapeake Bay. One older reporter had covered a lynching there in the 1940s. I spent many hot nights in Cambridge as tensions mounted between blacks marching for equal rights and enraged whites, restrained from violence only by the Maryland National Guard. It was the civil rights revolution in miniature; Cambridge even had a main thoroughfare called Race Street.

In one sense it was a story like the Cold War. A reporter trained to be objective told both sides, but it was obvious that there was a morally right side. Experiences like the Berlin Wall had left me in no doubt which side I was on in the Cold War. Here, watching white toughs swear at, spit on, and throw stones at fellow citizens they had grown up with again left me in no doubt.

One evening I was standing with a young black man named Freddie, watching a group of whites jeering and cursing. Freddie said, "You see that Hank over there? I grew up with him. He ate as much off my table as I did. My mom wiped his nose. He wore my clothes and he screwed my cousin, and when I walked up there today, you know what he said to me? 'You black son of a bitch!' "

I could witness some white intransigence in my own family. My grandmother, Daisy Neely Oxner, came to visit me in Washington, her first time there in more than half a century. I picked her up at National Airport and drove along the Potomac, pointing out the sights—Washington Monument, Lincoln Memorial. Daisy gave the memorial a quick glance, then half turned away in her seat, saying contemptuously, "That man Lincoln!" That was all she said, a century after the Civil War.

Her visit made me curious about her side of our family history. I had been given the middle name Breckenridge after her father, John Breckenridge Neely. He was descended from Neelys who emigrated from Northern Ireland to New York in the 1740s. Two John Neelys, father and son, fought in the Revolution and later settled in Virginia. Daisy's father moved to Tennessee and became a prominent builder of railroads and bridges. At his death, the *Chattanooga Times* said that "All over the South he was looked upon as a master in his line."

The *New York Times* printed a picture of Daisy as "a typical Southern Belle." After breaking her leg in a fall from her horse, she received beaux from a sofa on the landing of the house, each smitten young man climbing the stairs to lay a dozen long-stemmed roses in her lap.

Another story fascinated me as a child. Her father was ailing but had a contract to finish a section of railroad outside Atlanta, and the laborers had to be paid. From his sickbed he commanded Daisy to ride out and pay them. She did, carrying the gold coins in her skirt, dispensing them from the saddle while the workers said things like, "We knew honest John Neely would never let us down."

For reasons never explained to me, Daisy left her family and the South for good. She went off to Europe with an older woman companion of humorless temperament. In their three-year tour of France, Germany, and Italy they saw every opera, every picture in every museum and church, while staying in modest pensions and generally skimping on fun. Her daughter, Peggy, my mother, thought the experience had warped Daisy for life, making her sweetly southern socially but in private a mean-spirited vixen, or even, after great provocation, a BI, Peggy not wishing to say *bitch*. I can only assume it was their relationship that made my mother so anti-American.

When she returned from this cultural forced march, Daisy went to stay with an aunt in Baltimore. One day she noticed a handsome fellow on a horse passing the house, contrived to stop him, and fell in love. Warren Oxner was studying dentistry at Johns Hopkins. He graduated, they married and moved to Halifax—foggy, grim Halifax, about as far removed in climate and atmosphere from languid, magnolia-scented Chattanooga as she could get.

After Daisy left Washington, the Lincoln and Jefferson Memorials became temples I wanted repeatedly to visit. I often took visitors, usually at night. And I never failed to experience a mystical feeling, a religious emotion, the hair on my neck rising slightly, on reading again the stirring words inscribed. I had never experienced a comparable leap of the heart for any Canadian historical personage. No Canadian figure has ever inspired me like Jefferson or Lincoln.

Standing there, I could feel Lincoln's "mystic chords of memory" touching me, even though they were not officially my memories. And for all my skepticism of America, the better angels of her nature were certainly evident when Martin Luther King spoke there during the March on Washington later that summer, when the atmosphere of racial goodwill was palpable.

By the time of the march, I had been moved to the White House as a second correspondent to Vanocur, covering briefings, doing radio reports, and going on some of the weekend trips to Hyannis. There could not have been a greater contrast between sweltering evenings in a black church in Cambridge—listening to the civil rights anthems I now knew by heart, waving a funeral parlor fan to keep the sweat off my face—and the Kennedy compound in Hyannis.

Those weekends were routine by now for the White House Press Corps, which moved with accustomed ease into the Yachtsman Motor Inn—some with families—as though to their own cottages. I felt quite an outsider, unsure even what to wear, but again I encountered that delightful ease with which Americans let you slide into intimacy, to make you feel included. These reporters, some very senior, were willing to spend hours showing me the ropes.

Soon I was playing tennis with Kennedy's press secretary, Pierre Salinger, going for a cocktail cruise on the presidential yacht, the *Honey Fitz*, picking up policy background and gossip at meals, and, when there was news, reporting it.

Occasionally, Salinger would stage a Saturday news conference with the president to make a story for the Sunday papers. At one of these for the first time, I asked Kennedy a question, acutely nervous that he would think it too stupid to answer, vastly relieved when he responded civilly. No other public figure had inspired such awe in me, but I had come late, most of my colleagues having covered him from the 1960 campaign, and I brought some resistance to Kennedy. I have an instinctive aversion to being snowed: the more I hear everyone telling me how wonderful someone is, especially a politician, the more I'm inclined to doubt. And the publicity wind that blew around JFK seemed relentlessly favorable. His barometer always read high, in the heroic range. All his defeats appeared graceful, his victories magnanimous. So I looked for grounds to be skeptical of him and they were hard to find.

News tumbled out of his White House days in such profusion that reporters were always rushing to report it, or rushing with him somewhere in the world to make it. In making news, he displayed personal qualities universally admired: he appeared brave, handsome, confident, eloquent, intelligent, witty, virile; all packaged with the glint of sardonic humor and a faint wash of Celtic melancholy. Those closer to the man confirmed all these traits, adding the element of naked anger when he was crossed.

One Saturday in August, I was playing tennis with Salinger, who had a phone by the side of the court. A few games into our match it rang and he took a call from the president, who was furious over some negative reporting from Vietnam. His anger must have grown because the phone rang so often we had to abandon the match. After that he tried unsuccessfully to bully publishers into removing offending reporters, including David Halberstam, from Saigon.

I was half conscious of being used a little in Kennedy image-making on a weekend when I was part of the pool, the group of four reporters representing wire services, newspapers, magazines, and networks who travel with the president and share their observations with the full press corps later. At the end of the journey from Washington, our helicopter landed at the Kennedy compound and we got out to watch the president's helicopter land. It was a brilliant late afternoon in July. The white, shingled houses faced the sea across a lawn ending in sea grass and dunes.

Still new to all this, I thought it an odd convention the press has with the president compared with the practice in other countries. We are brought in to witness episodes in the president's life that elsewhere would be considered none of anyone's business. Of course, we witness only what they choose to show and there is calculation in that choice. Here I watched JFK being delivered safely into the loving arms of his adoring wife, children, parents, sisters, and brothers. Many years later, now aware of the president's obsessive philandering, I assume we were there as staged witnesses to marital fidelity and family values, in case of any whispers to the contrary. But at the time I was mostly dazzled by the spectacle of the very rich commuting on a Friday afternoon in summer.

Although far out of my reach financially, the summer life in Hyannis felt comfortable to me. I learned only years later that my great-grandfather had summered and invested there. But there was a lot I didn't know then.

Those brief but close-up glimpses of the Kennedys at work and play are burned into my memory with special intensity, like the black-and-white photographs that have become icons in the national consciousness.

I remember one moment when Air Force One arrived at Otis Air Force Base in Massachusetts. As the president came down the steps, John John and Caroline ran up to meet him. They walked away, Caroline holding her father's hand, and she used it to rub an itch on her nose. The moment was caught by a photographer and today when I see the picture here and there, all my own paternal emotions rush back to that moment.

My children, Cathy and Ian, were just the ages of Caroline and John Jr. They had been staying with my mother in Ottawa while I got settled and now they had come to live in the house I had rented in Vienna, Virginia. My mother agreed to come and look after them for a while. But with my constant traveling, it did not work well for her or me.

Soon after we moved in, Ian, then four, developed a sudden high fever. We found the name of a pediatrician and I called. His nurse told me to bring the child over. I was astounded. "The child is sick. He has a temperature of 103!" I shouted into the phone. "Oh, wrap him in a blanket and bring him over," she said.

Really angry at this seeming callousness, a metaphor for my lingering forebodings about the U.S., I complied, muttering to myself that in London, our overworked, modestly paid doctor in Britain's much-maligned "socialized medicine" had always come to the house.

· · ·

By summer's end 1963 it was obvious that our domestic arrangements were unfair to my mother, who was only fifty-six and needed her independence. Then my brother Hugh and his wife, Alison, offered to have my children live with them in Nova Scotia until I could straighten out my life. An enormously generous gesture, adding two more persons to their own two. So Cathy and Ian went to live with their cousins in Halifax, with the joy of snowy winters and cool summers by the sea. A few years later my mother married Donald Mackay, a widowed Halifax artist, whose charming daughter, Margot, thus became our stepsister.

I plunged on with my career, the personal emotions too overwhelming to be thoroughly analyzed, as they probably should have been, my now aggressive ambition driving me too rapidly for contemplation.

7

A CRASH COURSE IN AMERICA

*I*n September, NBC gave me a plum assignment, to cover Barry Goldwater, Kennedy's possible opponent in 1964, on a six-week tour of the U.S. Only three reporters came—Charlie Mohr of the *New York Times*, Walter Mears of the Associated Press, and I—so we got to know Goldwater and forged relationships before the journalist pack descended. It was relaxed, with few public events, as he sounded out key Republicans in states important to the presidential nomination.

While I had traveled widely in Europe and a little in Africa, it was a new experience to hopscotch a continent like this, daily leaps covering many states. It gave me a dream tour of the country, in one trip seeing more of the U.S. than I ever had seen of Canada. As we moved from New Hampshire to the Midwest, to

Florida, to California, the Northwest, and Texas, I felt a rising pleasure. The country offered such enormous variety—not only in geography and climate, but in the breadth of its political spectrum and the new personalities it bred. All that was stimulating for the journalist trying to establish some literacy in American politics. But the dazzling contrasts in scenery and regional cultures were a pleasure to the traveler in me. Half the fun of being a reporter is having the experiences tourists pay for: *huevos con chorizo* for breakfast in Tucson, sloppy barbecue in Dallas, stone crabs in Miami Beach.

I enjoy traveling not only to see great monuments and landmarks, but to witness how people make their lives in different landscapes and climates, and the instructive marks that leaves upon the land. The *pentimenti* of good husbandry. I carried that urge back from Europe, where I am always less amazed by the sublime in nature than by the patient industry of man that frames it. So while I admired the deserts and canyons of Arizona, glimpses of the Grand Tetons in Wyoming, the grandeur of the California coast at Monterey, they had an air of being worn by too many pairs of tourist eyes bused in for the dutiful glance, too much photographed. As jaded cameramen say when led to cliché shot, "You can see the tripod holes!"

But some landscapes immediately awaken an intimate response. I feel I know better who I am when that happens, as it did that year on seeing the artful domestic landscapes in New Hampshire. As we went from village to village, especially in winter, I couldn't see enough of those farmscapes, elegant colonial houses sprouting barns and outbuildings, all wearing uniform tints derived from eighteenth-century homemade paints—faded red from ox blood and milk, blue from blueberries—enclosed by stone walls and leafless sugar maples with a backdrop of dark spruce; each passing view awaiting a painter or a novelist to set some human mischief in these pristine, postcard scenes. They were part of the motive, ostensibly journalistic, that kept drawing me back to New Hampshire. And they still insist in my imagination, giving me messages I haven't yet quite decoded.

. . .

With Goldwater, we returned always to Arizona and what became a second home—the Camelback Inn in Scottsdale.

One night we flew with the senator to Mexico and the haunts of his youth in the border town of Nogales. In a restaurant where they treated him like a long-lost son, we had a great meal and a lot of margaritas. I was doing a television profile of the senator on that leg of the tour and an NBC cameraman and soundman were with me.

With NBC urging me to complete my citizenship application, and I complaisant about it (there were so many more important things happening, it seemed), I had agreed to spend the obligatory year inside U.S. borders. I remembered that only when we had to recross the border. The senator and his wife, Peggy, went through immigration, followed by the NBC crew. The INS officer said to the cameraman, "Where were you born?"

"NBC."

He asked the soundman, "Where were you born?"

"NBC."

He asked me, and "NBC" seemed the right answer. Goldwater was watching all this and kidded me for a long time that he had smuggled me back into the U.S.

We ended that evening with the senator, Peggy, and his journalist escort standing under the wing of his private plane at Phoenix airport, swigging from a bottle of tequila. Very informal. Very Barry.

Filming for the profile at his house outside Scottsdale, Goldwater showed the camera a grapefruit tree grafted so as to produce oranges and lemons as well. Such was the privileged life in Paradise Valley for the heir to a department store fortune, Air Force general, initiated blood brother of the Hopi Indians, early collector of their stunning *kachina* dolls, serious amateur photographer, cactus gardener, and insatiable ham radio guy.

Goldwater the compulsive gadgeteer had made a small artificial waterfall outside the bedroom with the sound miked in, and a flagpole equipped a photoelectric cell; at the dawn's early light his Stars and Stripes automatically went up the pole to descend at the twilight's last gleaming.

Politicians who become national figures inevitably are distillations, and exaggerations, of varied traits in the American character and personality. Goldwater was my first concentrated lesson in the informal, laconic, aw-shucks side of the national personality, typical of the easier-going West, content with intuitive judgments, impatient of detailed study, willing to tell it like it is when he got riled up.

While I had doubts about Goldwater as presidential material—too undisciplined, too willing to shoot from the hip verbally—I liked him personally. Sitting around in the evenings, when the senator had disappeared from view, we compared Goldwater and Kennedy. Which man would you rather be roped to if you were in a climbing and your life depended on it? We knew about JFK's heroism in the PT-109, but we all concluded Goldwater would be more selfless in a crunch.

At the end of that first Goldwater tour in early November 1963, I came back to Washington with a new sense of belonging, and I felt well dug in. I had given up the house in Virginia and moved into a sublet one-bedroom apartment in Foggy Bottom, close enough to walk to the White House, where I resumed my job as the number two correspondent. I really liked that part of Washington, the old trees erupting through red brick sidewalks, rows of Georgian or federal houses.

Autumn in Washington is a golden haze, progressing so stealthily that the piles of fallen yellow ginkgo leaves grow imperceptibly and the sun bathes it all in a warm, wistful glow. I loved all that, and short weekend trips into the Blue Ridge Mountains to see the dogwood leaves turning a passionate magenta and the sycamores dropping pale yellow-green. What it lacked in the drama of crisp nights and brilliant leaves of the Canadian or New England fall, it replaced with this graceful and knowing surrender; not the scarlet hussy jumping in to warm up a cold bed, but a Blanche Dubois languidly divesting. Always noticing the minutiae of changing seasons, I found that first Washington autumn a delicious and poignant spectacle.

On a weekend afternoon in mid-November, I was at the White House for a visit by the Black Watch Scottish regiment and their pipe band. It was a sparkling, crystal day. The president and Mrs. Kennedy were on the balcony of the south portico with the children on their laps as soldiers in Highland dress paraded, bagpipes skirling, a brave sight. I remember feeling perfectly content, happy to be where I was, part of all this, glancing now and then at the Kennedys and their children.

Surrounded by such grace and beauty, paid to observe a president who wielded American power with a rationality and grace that even the querulous allies admired, advancing rapidly in a career I had not chosen but found heady and rewarding, why would I not adore being in America?

In those years I prided myself on compartmentalizing my life, the personal efficiently partitioned off from the professional. I can see now how the two mingled and affected my behavior at every stage.

The crisis with Rosemarie was a year and a half behind us in November 1963. The professional who had been counseling her in London believed that our marriage was not savable, but to be sure, we should have a trial reunion. In my heart, from the first glimpse of her at Dulles Airport, I knew it was over. She said she thought so too but wasn't sure. She moved in with me and we tried to be kind to each other. There are few situations as tormented as living with someone who had been the great love and whom you no longer love, but you are two healthy people in your early thirties and you need the physical comfort the other can provide. Except that you don't want such overtures to be taken as a revival of love, because you know that has gone. But she is a delightful, intelligent, and worldly woman whom you don't want to hurt anymore. And you don't want to be hurt anymore yourself. And up in Nova Scotia are the two children, yours and hers. Their fate ticks like a nagging clock. The only relief was that each morning I had to walk over to the White House to do my job. Unfortunately, there were weekends with no assignments. I have never been more miserable.

In that mood I learned that Sander Vanocur was going to Hawaii to cover a high-level conference on the Vietnam War, so I would be the NBC correspondent on the Kennedys' trip to mend political fences in Texas.

The visits to San Antonio and Houston were rapturously received, and by the time we reached Fort Worth late Thursday night even the feuding Democrats were impressed enough with the Kennedy glamour to paper over their antipathies. One element in their success was Jackie Kennedy's new zest for campaigning.

The next morning I covered the breakfast at which she mischievously waited in the hotel kitchen to build suspense for her entrance, which caused a sensation. When the cheers died, the president said, "Two years ago, I introduced myself in Paris by saying that I was the man who had accompanied Mrs. Kennedy to Paris. I am getting somewhat the same sensation [he began to laugh and the crowd laughed, too] as I travel around Texas. Nobody wonders what Lyndon and I wear." That brought the house down, and I said to the NBC cameraman, Moe Levy, "Well, even if nothing else happens, we've got a story with Jackie."

We flew to Dallas, and as the motorcade formed up I ran for a seat at the front of the first press bus, seven cars behind the presidential limousine.

When the shots were fired, our bus was heading toward the Texas School Book Depository, about to turn left. I made the bus driver stop, got out, and, as he drove on, ran to the corner. The air was filled with screaming. I saw policemen and civilians running up the slope later known as "the grassy knoll." Believing they were chasing a gunman, I ran with them. We all stopped by the fence at the top. After a few seconds' hesitation, the police went over the fence and I did, too. I could see no one on the other side. Figuring I had better call NBC about the shots being fired, I ran along the top looking for a phone. The first building that looked as though it might have one was the Texas School Book Depository. As I ran up the steps, a young man in shirtsleeves came out. When I asked breathlessly for a phone, he said I'd better ask inside. I did and another young man himself on a phone pointed to an office. I got through to NBC in a few seconds, then waited agonizing seconds more because the news producer was tied up. When he came on, I recorded a bulletin saying that shots were fired as the presidential motorcade passed through downtown Dallas, and from my Reuters training, cautioned, "It is not known if the shots were directed at the president," and repeated it for emphasis. It was inconceivable to me that Kennedy had been hit.

Outside, a policeman stopped me as I left the building. As I was identifying myself, a small black boy of eight or nine came up and said, "Mister, I saw a man with a gun up there in that window." At the same moment a distracted woman asked, "Was he hit? Was he hit?" I said, "No, I'm sure he wasn't," but immediately, doubting my certainty, I rushed over to a motorcycle cop who was listening to his radio.

"Was he hit?"

"Yeah, hit in the head. They're taking him to Parkland Hospital."

The scene was chaotic. Police cars and motorcycles were screaming up, bouncing over curbs and through flower beds. Thousands of horns were beeping from traffic backed up on the streets feeding into Dealy Plaza.

Distraught because I was supposed to be covering the president and he was miles away, I ran across the plaza until I found a street with traffic moving and stopped the first car that came by. I opened the door and said, "I'll give five dollars to take me to Parkland Hospital." The young man said okay and I got in, when he asked, "What's going on?" I said the president had been shot and he said he'd heard that on the radio. "Well turn it on!" I shouted. He said it was in the backseat, a transistor. He had heard that the president had been shot, turned off the radio, and dumped it in the backseat.

As he raced toward the hospital, I pounded on the guy's arm, saying, "Never mind the traffic lights. Go as fast as you can. NBC will pay for any fines." But all police cars we saw were flashing by, sirens wailing, back toward Dealy Plaza. We stopped at a gas station where I made another call to NBC to report the president's injuries. Then we raced on to Parkland, arriving soon after the pool car that had been at the front of the motorcade. The two press buses had been diverted to the site where Kennedy was to have spoken.

Inside the emergency room waiting area I found an idle pay phone and called NBC again. I kept that phone the rest of the afternoon, with interns holding it when I went to get more information about Kennedy's condition, Lyndon Johnson's departure, confirmation of the president's death, and finally Jackie leaving in her blood-spattered pink suit, one of her hands possessively resting on the coffin as they wheeled it out.

Our communications technology was so primitive that NBC could not patch my call through to the flash studio in New York, where Chet Huntley, Bill Ryan, and Frank McGee were reporting. On anniversaries now they often run the tape of that broadcast, showing these big news stars of their time trying to put the earpiece of a phone near a microphone to put my voice on the air. Finally they settled for me delivering a sentence and McGee repeating it, which gave me a little time to think.

When it was reported that a man who worked at the book depository had been arrested, it passed through my mind that he might have been coming out of the building as I went in, but I had no strong visual memory of the man; my attention had been totally focused on finding a phone. That evening I went to Dallas police headquarters and saw Lee Harvey Oswald twice at close range as they paraded him through the throng of reporters, one eye bruised from the scuffle at his arrest. I heard him say, "I'm just a patsy", but I did not recognize him.

Eighteen months later, William Manchester called me with a question. He was finishing his book *The Death of a President* and wanted to confirm that it was Oswald I had stopped and asked for a phone. He said he had been over the ground second by second; he had timed my first call to NBC at four minutes after the shots and was 95 percent convinced it was Oswald I had spoken to. He told me, which I had not known, that the Secret Service had interviewed Oswald that evening. As he left the book depository, Oswald said, a tall blond Secret Service man ran up the steps and asked him for a phone. No Secret Service agent did enter the building. I was tallish, blond with a short haircut, and wore a gray suit with a White House press badge, and Manchester believed that Oswald mistook me for a Secret Service man. In the book he states that as Oswald left the building, he talked to NBC's Robert MacNeil.

I have been asked many times what I believe about the assassination. And I say, usually to the questioner's disappointment, that I believe the Warren Commission conclusion that Oswald acted alone until someone comes up with hard evidence to disprove it. My one open question is: Why did Dallas policemen— probably as experienced as anyone in hearing gunshots echoing off tall buildings—run up the grassy knoll? Belief that a shot came from there fuels many conspiracy theories, but no one has produced conclusive evidence.

The curious thing is that, earlier that day on the way from the airport into Dallas, very tired, I had a momentary daydream in which someone took a shot at the president, I got out of the bus and chased him, then woke up, told myself to get serious, and forgot it. Yet, when the actual shots were fired, I did exactly what I had in the daydream, as though a psychic plan had been programmed there.

The day after the assassination I went with a camera crew to retrace all of Oswald's movements that I could, visiting his rooming house, his bedroom, talking to his landlady, following his route south, and interviewing witnesses who saw him shoot police officer Tippet, whose blood still stained the pavement. We filmed the shoe store where he ducked in to hide from a police car and the movie theater where he was arrested. It was still showing the John Wayne movie *War Is Hell*, and we sat in the seat Oswald had occupied to get his perspective on the screen.

On Monday of the funeral in Washington we were filming at the grassy knoll, which had become a small shrine of flowers and notes, perhaps the beginning of a phenomenon that, with television coverage feeding back an action to be imitated, has since become bizarre, as witness the acres of flowers brought in mourning for Princess Diana.

There were only a few flowers in Dallas, and we filmed people looking at them. An elderly man sat down on the stone parapet and put his transistor radio beside him. At that moment the Black Watch pipe band I had seen at the White House was passing in the funeral procession in Washington. Instantly I found myself sobbing. For three days I had felt numb, fixated on the story and how to cover it. Now the sound of the bagpipes caused all the stifled feelings to surface.

My emotions remained raw for weeks. Back in Washington, I found myself depressed in a way I had never known. My disposition is usually optimistic and cheerful, but I could not stop myself from thinking, What is rotten in this country? What spoor of violence could provide the psychological context for such an act? I was so appalled by the act that I convinced myself that the society had bred evil. So much virulent hatred of Kennedy: What had he done to incite such murderous anger and paranoia? Why could it not be accommodated, ventilated within the democratic institutions?

And this was the country I had so enthusiastically attached myself to? I couldn't imagine this happening in Britain or Canada. Did I really belong here?

It sickened me to hear the positive chatter on television, with pundits echoing each other . . . how well the system worked . . . continuity was assured . . . the Constitution preserved . . . blah blah blah. I was in a deep funk, obviously deepened by the depressing personal situation between Rosemarie and me. I weathered it by going for long walks around Washington, frequently visiting the Lincoln and Jefferson Memorials for comfort or reassurance, and reading Georges Simenon. A bookstore in Georgetown had a good supply of his Maigret detective series, so redolent of Paris, so acute in their psychology, spare in their prose—and so far removed from stricken Washington.

With the help of friends we weathered the Christmas holidays, then Rosemarie and I agreed to divorce. She waited in Washington until that was complete and then moved back to London. The children were still in Halifax.

And then NBC dispelled my gloom by giving me the Goldwater beat for the full presidential year. For the rest of 1964, I followed his campaign, with occasional breaks to cover features stories for *The Huntley-Brinkley Report*—the military coup in Brazil, a visit to Devil's Island, a hurricane lashing New Orleans.

With Goldwater I attended thirteen Lincoln Day dinners in

different cities, each lending its own flavor to the flag ceremony, invocation, the mundanities that give politics its heart and soul. Often during the Pledge of Allegiance I would catch the senator's or Peggy's eye from the floor next to the stage where reporters gathered and fancy a little ironic smile. National reporters usually ignored such rituals, often to the disgust of conservative audiences, but the Goldwaters were amused that a British-Canadian, as they saw it, was covering this campaign for an American network. One of his speechwriters was Karl Hess, then a very right-wing fellow, who later did a 180, as they say of snowboarders, and became a late-'60s child of the left. One night, long before this radical conversion, he and I were sitting together in the campaign plane chatting through the night. Finally we landed somewhere at dawn and Hess said to me, "How come NBC appointed an alien, atheist, communist to cover Barry Goldwater?" Goldwater's own verdict, inscribed on a photo I prized, was "To a fair and objective man."

Goldwater's personality was lighter and better humored than the rhetoric put together for him. He sounded harsh and uncompromising uttering lines like "Extremism in the defense of liberty is no vice. . . ." (which stunned moderate Republicans at the San Francisco convention), but the tone of delivery sounded unlike the man, who was easygoing and funny.

He often referred to his mixed religion (father Jewish, mother Episcopalian) by saying, "I went to a restricted golf course and when they said I couldn't play, I said, 'Well, I'm only half Jewish, can I play nine holes.'" That led the humorist Harry Golden to remark, "I always knew the first Jewish president of the United States would be an Episcopalian."

That campaign was my first exposure to the strange and

sometimes rabid distemper on the American right, which has seemed only to grow as conservatives have captured the center of U.S. politics.

One Goldwater campaign stop was in Paradise, California, a small community of fruit growers nestled prosperously in a lovely valley of almond and apricot trees in bloom. We came on a spring morning, the air perfumed, the light shining with special grace, like descending into Shangri-la. But the Goldwater supporters that year, like so many in California, John Birchers and others, were people unhappy in paradise: angry, suspicious, furiously antigovernment. They behaved like the caricature of Americans that often passes for coverage of the U.S. in some European newspapers.

In one Orange County campaign stop, Goldwater was speaking with reporters gathered by the stage in that attitude of insolent languor by which the press communicates it has heard it all before, but dutifully takes notes in case a bombshell drops—and Goldwater didn't disappoint in that department.

Ed Nellor, his press secretary, came up and whispered to me, "A guy just dragged me outside to tell me, there are men in there with notebooks and they're writing down every word the senator says!" Whether the man was truly paranoid or just naive, taking close notes was not always a kindness to Goldwater, who could be startlingly candid; like saying casually during the New Hampshire primary that NATO field commanders should have tactical nuclear weapons and the authority to use them.

That provided a few megatons of copy and inspired the Democrats' notorious daisy petal commercial. It was shown only once and withdrawn but became legendary: a pretty little girl plucking petals from a daisy saying, "He loves me, He loves me not," while a male voice counts down, 10, 9, 8 . . . until there is a blinding flash and a mushroom cloud. Goldwater had no one to blame but himself for the impression that he would be careless with nuclear warfare just when the first restraints on testing were being debated.

He gave Democratic commercial makers another visual gift by suggesting that the northeastern United States be sawed off and allowed to float out to sea: TV spots then showed someone literally sawing New England off a plywood map.

But Goldwater's candor sprang from a place in his character that did not send every utterance through the expediency and political censorship loop.

·   ·   ·

By the time Lyndon Johnson swamped Goldwater in November 1964, I had been to all forty-eight contiguous states and sampled at close hand a cross-section of American character—the idealism, the thirst for authenticity and principled leadership, the paranoia, the endearing idiocies and excesses that politics create. They did not inspire the hostile feelings they probably would have if read about in Europe or even friendly Canada. American humanity needed to be tasted, to be encountered in the flesh, because in the abstract, from afar, it was so often, and so easily, ridiculed.

When I saw my journalist friends as bemused by the ridiculous and moved by the serious moments as I was, I felt more and more integrated, was beginning to feel I belonged. One incident shows how embedded in groupthink I had become and how much of the outsider's ironic distance I had lost.

Charlie Mohr of the *New York Times* had become a friend.

Charlie was often called the reporter's reporter, widely traveled and full of stories, the best kind of companion when much of one's entertainment is waiting around (often eating and drinking) for the candidate. Because Charlie had just come back from Vietnam, we talked a lot about the U.S. role there. He had quit *Time* magazine because the Luce mind-set would not accept his skeptical reporting from Saigon.

By midsummer 1964, I was spending some time covering the Johnson White House in gaps between Goldwater campaign events, and I thought I had a clear idea of how the administration was handling the war. Between the conventions I took ten days' vacation to visit a friend in Trinidad. One evening we drove from Port of Spain to the city of San Fernando to attend a political meeting, where some passionate Marxists attacked the United States and the crowd loved it. Driving back to Port of Spain, we gave two of the young talkers a lift and they carried on their argument: LBJ was on the verge of escalating to much greater war in Vietnam, American imperialism was on the march, and so on. Knowing I came from Washington, they politely asked what I thought. With great assurance I said they were wrong. Lyndon Johnson was too passionate about completing unfulfilled parts of President Roosevelt's domestic agenda to risk seeing his legacy flushed away down some sinkhole in Southeast Asia. When he said "I seek no wider war," he meant it. They could rely on it. Perhaps I had begun to pick up the punditry virus. There I was with uncommon access to Washington information, and the next year proved them quite right and me wrong.

Exposure to LBJ let me experience another unforgettable slice of American character, manically ambitious and manipulative, overbearing and boorish, yet charming and persuasive, wantonly boastful yet devastatingly insecure, mawkish at times, inspiring at others—all present to a degree that made his presence over-whelming.

One encounter showed many of these traits. On a busy day, when I had switched to the LBJ campaign for perspective, I was in the pool aboard Air Force One as we dashed across the country from Indiana to Texas to California. Johnson asked me and Frank Cormier of the AP to come back to the bedroom. He was sweat-ing profusely and told us to sit on the twin beds as he took off all his clothes down to his shorts, toweled dry, and redressed in a clean shirt, suit, and tie, talking all the while. Then he sat down be-side me and continued for an hour or so, emphasizing his points by tapping me on the thigh. Since his hands were huge, his tap was a heavy jab and I had a bruise for a couple of weeks afterward.

He wanted us to know that if we trusted him, LBJ could put us right with our bosses. His pitch went something like this:

"Cormier, you don't want to be White House correspondent for the AP all your life. You want to be one of those big fancy edi-tors up there in New York. And MacNeil, you don't want to be just a correspondent for NBC News. You want to be a big guy making the big money like Huntley and Brinkley. Well, here's how you go about it."

He learned over intimately, as if drawing us into a real con-spiracy.

"Now what impresses your bosses up there in the AP and NBC? Is it you guys reporting what everyone else reports? No. What really makes them pay attention is when you have some-thing the other reporters don't have. When you have inside infor-mation. When you know about a story before anyone else does. When you have a scoop. Now you fellas are good reporters and you're smart. You play it straight with me and I'll see that both of you get lots of little bits of information, special information. That'll make those guys up there in New York think you're the smartest sons of bitches they've ever seen."

Then he went on for the rest of the flight, punching my leg to drive home the message, selling us ideas he said no one knew about yet, like his ambition to desalinate seawater: "You look down there you can see there's a awful lot of these United States that's dry. Water could become the greatest problem, the greatest crisis this country ever has to face. But I'm determined to do something about it. . . ." And on and on, leaving me wondering how many other reporters the President of the United States had taken the time to cajole like this.

. . .

In 1965, two things happened that temporarily cemented me even more firmly into American life.

After the election, *The Huntley-Brinkley Report* again sent me off on a series of feature stories, a fabulous job in which I traveled with a film crew (this time friends from London) doing one feature a week, minidocumentaries, on expatriate Cuban influence in Spain, Britain's precarious hold on Gibraltar, and the emerging European Common Market. Then Winston Churchill entered his final illness and I went to London to help cover his death and funeral. I had been present in the House of Commons during some of his last appearances, very moved to see this frail old man creeping into the chamber where his words that had electrified the free world still echoed.

I did an atmospheric feature on old men digging his grave in the village of Bladon, like two characters from Shakespeare, and another in his underground World War II war room, preserved but in those days closed to the public. NBC ran that piece on three different programs. I also helped narrate his funeral, all the while feeling how pleasant it was to be back in Europe.

I had gone to the U.S. in '63 with the notion, at least in my head, that NBC was seasoning me to become a bureau chief in Paris, Berlin, or London, but that was not what they had in mind.

．　．　．

Back in Washington, I began dating Jane Doherty, who worked in the NBC newsroom. She was ten years younger than I, cheerful, enthusiastic, and pretty. We fell in love and decided to be married at the end of May. Besides marriage, she was willing to share the parenting of Cathy and Ian.

For NBC I was doing odd assignments, civil rights hearings in Mississippi, one of the Gemini space shots at Cape Canaveral, then the march on Selma, Alabama. Because several locations were involved, the network had me anchoring in a studio in Montgomery to coordinate reports from several correspondents. A friend in New York called to congratulate me about a story in the *Herald Tribune*, saying I was to be transferred to New York to be coanchor of a new Saturday news program with Ray Scherer in Washington. The reporter even had the title, *The Scherer-MacNeil Report*, although no one had spoken to me about it.

So I moved to New York, which I had yearned for in the 1950s, and began anchoring both the network program and a new local one-hour newscast, *The Sixth Hour News*. That resulted in my picture going up in Times Square, roughly overlooking the spot where thirteen years before the inner voice had told me to give up acting. In fact, the *Sixth Hour* job was really like acting since there was little journalism in my role. I wrote a short summary of foreign news, for the rest I read what others had written. Often I had time to read only a few pages ahead during commercials and had to take a wild leap at unfamiliar place names, often getting them wrong. Residents of Ma-MAR-oneck heard it pronounced Mam-a-RO-neck. I disliked the role but the ratings rose, pulling ahead of the CBS local station, and I was well paid.

Jane and I were married and Cathy and Ian, now eight and six, came to live with us in a pleasant apartment near Gracie Mansion. In January 1967 our daughter Alison was born, so I now had an American wife and daughter and two British kids, three of us with green cards.

The Scherer-MacNeil Report prospered and I was able to do some actual reporting for it, for example a week in Israel on the eve of the 1967 war. But travel meant being absent from the *Sixth Hour* and skipping my radio essays three times a week. In those days one's income derived partly from salary and partly from "talent fees" for each sponsored program you appeared on. If you were absent, no fee, a system that easily produced mixed motives. I finally came to realize that anchor meant being dug in, rarely getting out into the field. That gradual understanding made me unhappy.

I was able to work on many specials and a couple of documentaries, including an early look at the political paralysis surrounding gun control. But most of my time was spent preparing to read copy on camera, which was what I thought I did least well. It was copy I hadn't written and couldn't write because of the mechanics of tape editing and scripting, although I could advise and consent. I began to long for the autonomy I'd enjoyed in the field, being my own boss as long as I turned in pieces they liked.

But another unhappiness was creeping up on me: the Vietnam War. The prophecies of the young Marxists in Trinidad had proved correct; so had the ironic observations of some Republicans: "They told me if I voted for Goldwater we'd be mining Haiphong Harbor and defoliating the jungle—and I did—and we have!"

I grew increasingly disturbed by what seemed obvious: the administration was either deceiving itself or deceiving the nation. We now know it was both. In my radio commentaries I had some leeway for interpretive comment, and my skepticism leaked through those scripts. But mine was a small voice alongside the naked disbelief of journalists in Saigon, the incredulity of allied governments, and the antiwar protests that were beginning at home. I was given two chances to go to Vietnam, once for a Christmas-with-the-troops broadcast for WNBC, which I thought too sentimental and refused—wrongly. I should have gone and made what I could of the chance. In December '66, NBC asked me to go to Saigon as correspondent for six months. This time I refused because my wife was about to give birth. But I began to feel the war personally, appalled that the bodies were being, I thought, almost smuggled home at the rate of about a hundred a week while life continued almost as though it weren't happening.

Our own coverage began to make me uneasy. Because it necessarily followed U.S. initiatives—actions launched, communists killed—it gave plausibility to the American line unless a reporter really stuck his neck out, as Morley Safer did for CBS. His report on Marines torching a Vietnamese village caused an uproar in the White House, which tried to smear him by investigating his roots in Canada and implying he was a communist sympathizer. Few incidents so graphically conveyed the futility or inherent contradictions in a war, in which we often appeared to be destroying Vietnam in order to save it.

I knew we were sanitizing the war because the reality of the pictures we received often violated the taste conventions established for a news program at suppertime. We rejected scenes of a young American screaming in agony because both lower legs had been blown away in misdirected fire from American artillery. Below the knee, his legs were tatters of bloody pulp and he was clawing, biting the earth as though trying to eat his way into it. Too raw, we decided. Another time we rejected shots of U.S. soldiers cutting ears off dead Vietcong as souvenirs. Not for suppertime, we decided, I in full agreement. But keeping the war within our taste parameters in effect helped the administration make it acceptable. Eventually, of course, some images smashed through the conventions and the taste threshold was lowered. Six months after we recoiled from the shots of ears as souvenirs, similar shots appeared on the *CBS Evening News*. The still picture of the little Vietnamese girl running naked in terror from a napalm attack, and the execution of a bound Vietcong with a point-blank pistol shot to the temple were examples that are now part of everyone's visual memory of Vietnam, like the piles of civilians massacred at My Lai. And of course, the more such images turned American civilian opinion against the war, the more the Pentagon and politicians blamed the media, especially television, for the eventual defeat. Today their heirs in the Pentagon and White House are exercising far more restrictive control over what military action they allow the cameras to see.

I privately admired the independent line Canada walked during Vietnam. The government permitted several thousand Canadians to volunteer and fight with American forces; it also granted asylum in Canada to thousands of Americans who refused to fight. There are no definitive figures, but one researcher, studying census data, concluded that nearly sixty thousand Americans took up residence in Canada, about half of them women. Many went home under Jimmy Carter's amnesty, but many liked Canadian society and stayed permanently. Some see Canada as a place of refuge from extreme American behavior. In Margaret Atwood's novel *The Handmaid's Tale*, Canada is considered a place to escape to from an America ruled by a totalitarian fundamentalistic theocracy.

Incidentally, one of those who made Canada her postwar home was Kim Phuc, the girl in the iconic napalm photo. After undergoing seventeen surgeries for her war injuries, she married, became a born-again Christian, and lives in Ajax, Ontario.

Eventually my unhappiness with the meaning of the war coverage combined with other discontents to give me a critical perspective on television journalism. That led indirectly to the founding of *The MacNeil-Lehrer NewsHour* on PBS—but that was long in the future.

In the fall of 1966, I was distracted by the off-year elections. NBC had assigned me to cover the governors' races on election night; to do that credibly I felt I had to go out and cover some actual races. That was made simpler because I was no longer anchoring the local news.

After I had done it for a year, WNBC actually volunteered to pay me more—something almost unheard-of—because the ratings were ahead of Jim Jensen's on WCBS. Astonished, I asked my agent to find out what Jensen was getting. It turned out to be twice what WNBC was paying me so, more amused than serious, I said, "Ask for that!" He did and I got bounced off the show. They never said why and I was too relieved to ask.

I covered governors' races in Arkansas, New York, and, most instructively, Ronald Reagan's bid in California. Pat Brown, the Democratic governor, had mounted a reelection campaign with ads attacking Reagan as an actor, a shortsighted strategy in a state that was mecca to actors, with politics more media-dominated and voters less committed to party than anywhere else in the country. One TV commercial said, "Remember, it was an actor that killed Abraham Lincoln." Any doubts I had about Reagan as a presidential candidate were dispelled the first time I saw him demonstrate the platform mastery that carried him to the White House.

Election nights were big events, when the network news departments showed their muscle, hoping to lure new viewers to their nightly news anchors. At NBC, Huntley and Brinkley would give an overall picture, then the producers would "whip round" the other desks for updates on the Senate, House, and governors. They would come to each of us for two minutes, signaling in advance which races so your commentary would match their graphics. I would have thirty seconds each for four governor's races, not much time in which to run the latest figures, throw in a little background, and add a little color, personality trait, or humor. NBC News distinguished itself from CBS in those days by encouraging the little ironic twist, deriving from the popular style of David Brinkley. One's ability to add such embroidery to the bare facts, and not sound frantic in the few seconds available, was part of how your abilities were measured "up there." It's no small feat to spit out such grace notes while playing the core melody.

To prepare, I had spent hours with political scientists augmenting the material I had gathered in the field. One of these academics thought it interesting that liberal Democrats in California were apparently sitting on their hands, in effect giving Reagan an easy victory over Pat Brown. It reminded the professor of the Social Democrats in Germany who had acquiesced in Hitler's election as chancellor, convinced that he would rapidly self-destruct and they would step in. *Nach Hitler uns* ("After Hitler us") was the slogan. In a moment of bad judgment, I used one of my short segments to tell that anecdote, with the result that thousands of viewers thought I was calling Reagan Hitler and jammed NBC switchboards across the nation to complain.

Another gaffe provoked an on-air argument with Brinkley. Reporting that Spiro Agnew was running well in Maryland against a more conservative candidate, I noted on air that Montgomery County adjoining the District of Columbia—home to many Washingtonians, including David Brinkley—often voted more liberal than other Maryland counties.

Brinkley swung around and said, "How do you know how I voted?" I began explaining—I didn't know, hadn't meant to imply, was just explaining the character of the county—but Brinkley was enjoying himself and kept on, "I thought we had a secret ballot in this country. . . . The privacy of the voting booth." It went back and forth several times, till the producers moved it on. My slips earned a box in *Time*, no reprimand from NBC, and a generous note from Brinkley. But they taught me that a little knowledge plus a desire to show off was dangerous.

In the control room after the broadcast I was greeted by Paul Fox, then head of BBC 1, the British Broadcasting Corporation's first network. He slapped me on the back and said, "Robin, why don't you come back to Britain and work for us?" I laughed but he'd planted a seed.

. . .

Another fascinating political assignment was to follow Richard Nixon's campaign that fall for Republican congressional candidates as a warm-up for his presidential run two years later. Nixon had metabolized his two traumatic losses, the presidency to Kennedy and the California governorship to Pat Brown, by portraying them in his book *Six Crises* as tests of character. Before the trip, a private briefing was arranged at Nixon's apartment and I brought my wife, Jane, to have a second opinion of the man. Although I carried a full set of received prejudices about Nixon, I determined to start with a clean slate.

We met in his study, where jade and ivory elephants paraded across the mantelpiece. On his desk was a knight in shining armor. Although the apartment felt cold and unlived in, the man himself was more personable than his reputation suggested. This Nixon was confident, expansive, even garrulous. And his intellectual performance impressed me. He went through all sixty-one congressional districts he would visit, naming incumbent and challenger, the political statistics, some subtle background, and probable outcome—all from memory, no notes. He predicted Republicans would pick up forty seats; on election day they gained forty-seven.

A few national reporters followed Nixon that fall, that seemingly reborn Nixon, uncharacteristically affable and accessible to the press, his often caricatured scowl and five o'clock shadow vanished, his demeanor charming when viewed on color television, just then becoming common, a fascinating contrast with his visage on black-and-white.

His professionalism was impressive. He could ad-lib a thirty-second or one-minute TV commercial and come in to the second, in one take. No retakes needed. And he had endless patience with the numbing drudgery of candidate life. They would line up supporters eager to be photographed with him, and Nixon would grin, shake hands, wait for the click, drop the hand, reignite the smile, shake the new hand . . . by the hundreds.

And why, after this stimulating immersion in American politics and the promise of more in the future, did it all suddenly turn sour? Something working at an unconscious level was driving me.

Sometime after the election I had a career talk with the NBC News brass and asked what my future was. One of them said, "Well, you're never going to be Huntley or Brinkley," and I said I'd never imagined I would. What I hoped for was a posting back overseas where I could be a reporter again, perhaps a bureau chief. They said that wasn't in the cards. They wanted me to stay and develop as an anchorman, which should make me happy since it was what so many others would die for, or words to that effect.

I left their office and impulsively wrote to the BBC exec, Paul Fox. If I did come to work there, what would I do? He promptly offered a job on *Panorama*, the BBC's weekly current affairs program, which predated *60 Minutes* and enjoyed similar prestige. I would be one of a handful of featured reporters able to cover the whole globe with long magazine pieces. My heart told me instantly to say yes, but I paused to be sensible, especially with a baby due any moment. When she (Alison) arrived safely, I told NBC what I was considering, and they countered by offering me one of four featured reporters' spots (they called them the "four horsemen") on *The Huntley-Brinkley Report*, a chance to do the roaming features I had enjoyed before. It was a serious offer but my back was up, I said no, and accepted the BBC offer. Many colleagues and friends thought it was not a rational decision, especially in financial terms; the BBC would pay about a third of what I was making in New York. But intuitively I felt my destiny did not lie with NBC.

I liked America, where my life had been so dramatically restarted in four years, but I felt another of those moments of clear certainty: I do not belong here, and I grabbed the chance to go back to London. I quit NBC and spent the summer working on a book about television and politics.

The Ford Foundation had just funded a two-year experiment called the Public Broadcast Laboratory (PBL) to make a national network on Sunday evenings as an alternative to commercial TV. They offered me a retainer to work for them overseas while at the BBC. My chronic freelancer's anxiety resurfaced and I accepted, also a fateful decision.

8

SEEING AMERICA FROM BRITAIN

Paradoxically I spent much of the next few years at the BBC back in the U.S., experiencing alongside Americans the traumas of the late sixties and early seventies, but now as an intimate and outside observer combined.

Reporting from a foreign country requires a different mindset from journalism within the nation. The foreign correspondent must play a subtle game of fitting new facts to his listeners' (in this case British) well-rooted expectations about the American story, while simplifying and interpreting rather heavily.

First, though, I had to reorient myself in British politics, and Jane and the children to a life in London vastly different from that in New York. Shortsightedly, I had agreed to pay to move our furniture across the Atlantic. That plus London's cost of living and taxes quickly ate up the BBC salary and my freelance earnings. Soon the money situation seemed very tight. Having arrived rather grandly on the liner *France*, we found ourselves in a rented house in Hampstead without the cash for a bottle of gin. Providentially my immediate boss, David Webster, turned up with some vodka and we survived, but the domestic adjustments were infinitely more difficult than the professional.

I rejoiced in the stimulating BBC atmosphere. Most of my colleagues on *Panorama* had been at Oxford or Cambridge (impressing the residual colonial snob in me) and three had been presidents of the Union, the debating club. Apart from the intellectual tone, the quality of such basic ingredients of television as the filming, sound recording, editing, and mixing were of a standard found at NBC only on the most prestigious documentaries.

The first stories took me out into the British regions—profiles of the Labor Party prime minister, Harold Wilson, and his Conservative Party rival, Edward Heath. Both parties had factions unhappy with their leadership, and we documented this in films that preceded live studio interviews. One source of Labor restiveness was a progressive closing of unproductive coal mines in Cumberland, near the Lake District. That was another magic landscape for me, rich in literary associations, most powerfully the children's novels of Arthur Ransome. We had free time to climb in the hills, drink fine bitter, and play darts, games so fiercely competitive we took the dartboard to our rooms after the bar closed.

Outside a pub on a Sunday, one craggy miner told us, "If they close this bloody pit, the bloody Labor Party's buggered," a level of saltiness we wouldn't have aired on NBC. We ran it on a big screen that Prime Minister Wilson watched, puffing on his pipe, but looking as though he'd bite the stem off when the miner's remark soared out to millions of homes.

The Heath profile involved film and commentary about how awkward his manner was with ordinary voters. The next day the conservative *Daily Mail*'s front-page banner headline read "Heath Pilloried on TV." No British leader ever submitted to that format again. I reveled in the freedom to broadcast such trenchant material. In the clubbiness of British public life, broadcasters and politicians were on a first-name basis, and politics was something of a parlor game until someone's ox was gored too deeply. But I found the mood at the publicly financed BBC refreshingly unreverential toward politicians.

The BBC appetite for American politics seemed insatiable that year and, as I was fresh from America, it made sense that I should cover it for *Panorama*. The more deeply I was immersed, the more fascinated I became, and the freedom to be quite interpretive (the distance of the foreign correspondent) added to the journalistic pleasure.

The New Hampshire primary was the key battleground in the 1968 presidential race, with the antiwar movement led by Senator Eugene McCarthy picking up enough followers, especially among the young, to convince President Johnson to withdraw. We covered the funeral of a U.S. Navy man, Ronald Keller, age nineteen, whose body had just been returned from Vietnam. When we asked his father if we might film the burial, he agreed, saying, "It'll give Ron's death some meaning." It said a lot that his government had provided no meaning. We filmed on a brilliant February day, in a snowy churchyard, the fresh grave a brown wound in the pristine setting, with its clapboard church and little U.S. flags on the graves of veterans of other wars. The seventeen-year-old widow, black-veiled, almost carried to the graveside, the military honor guard, their rifle shots echoing in the frozen air, the folding of the Stars and Stripes, were all parts of a ritual seared into the nation's memory by the Kennedy funeral. Now the folded flag was handed to this plump teenager, turned widow. When the funeral party left, a bulldozer revved up, settled its blade behind the pile of fresh earth, and filled in the grave with one thump. In the cutting room we used the voices of McCarthy, Nixon, and surrogates for Lyndon Johnson on the soundtrack, as though plucking them out of the broadcasts that filled the air. The film closed with the bulldozer.

Besides being shown on the BBC, the film was broadcast over U.S. public television stations—without the bulldozer. They thought it too brutal. I thought the film symbolic and accurate: politicians yakking away while uncomprehending families buried their dead. I was able to report more deeply, more tellingly, for a foreign broadcaster than I had done for NBC, although when I got back to Britain, my American wife, Jane, was upset: "How can you say such things about my country!"

Later she became angrier about the war than I. When our son Will was born in October 1970, we registered the birth with the U.S. embassy and he acquired an American passport. A year later, when the Nixon plan to end the war brought more escalation, Jane took the passport to the embassy in Grosvenor Square and threw it at them, saying, "You're not having my son for your filthy wars!"

As 1968 advanced and America's traumas mounted, we felt lucky to be living in Britain because the whole world outside seemed to be coming apart. American society was growing more violent and dislocated; after the Tet offensive, the Vietnam War looked more pointless but the killing continued; in France, riots and street protests toppled President de Gaulle; Czechoslovak gestures of independence were crushed by Soviet tanks; and a grue-some civil war raged in Nigeria.

. . .

I heard of the assassination of Martin Luther King on the radio in our Hampstead bedroom and within hours was flying to Atlanta. We were allowed to film beside his open coffin, his wounds invisible, his face serene, as hundreds of weeping people filed by. This too represented the character of America: soaring idealism and inspired leadership inciting murder, then more savagery as infuriated blacks looted and burned in Washington, D.C.

I had been with King several times, once beside him in a dense mass packed in the lobby of a church in Birmingham, Alabama, while a white mob raged outside, preventing us from leaving. I noticed King's stillness. Everyone was nervous and impatient, uncomfortable to be so crowded together. He showed none of that. For more than an hour he waited, his face as impassive as it looked now in his coffin.

Another time, in Memphis, Tennessee, I went with a cameraman to get King's reaction the night Medgar Evers, another civil rights leader, was shot. We knocked on the door of King's motel room. Through the cheap door we could hear rustling movements and we exchanged knowing looks. We'd heard stories of King's womanizing. We may have heard them because FBI Director J. Edgar Hoover was wiretapping his rooms and leaking the results to discredit King. More interesting American character there.

Eventually, in his shirtsleeves, King opened the door just wide enough to slip through into the hall, closing it behind him. Then he answered our questions, with that same mask of impassivity.

He was in the middle of an answer when I heard the faint clicking that meant the end of the film was running over the camera spockets. King heard it too and stopped speaking.

I asked him to finish the thought, but he said, "You're out of film."

"Yes but I can write it," I said, holding up my notebook.

He shook his head and excused himself to go back into the room. This media savvy was quintessentially American. And whatever was going on in that motel room was none of my business. No insights into American character: just human nature.

King was already so legendary in England that they carried hours of his funeral. The BBC practice was to let one reporter shape the commentary, rather than cut back and forth to many voices as American networks do. So I broadcast the entire King funeral from New York. After working unslept for forty-eight hours, we went to a restaurant in Rockefeller Center. At the bar I drank a martini and then walked over to the table and was waiting to sit down when a colleague said, "I think you'd better go home, old chap," and I fell flat on my face. They took me to the hotel and put me to bed and I knew nothing until the next day.

. . .

In May, *Panorama* sent me to France to cover the strikes and demonstrations that led to the resignation of President de Gaulle, the police baton charges and tear gas attacks unable to suppress the uprising. While students took over the Odéon Theater near the Sorbonne for a first aid post and cut down some of the noble plane trees in the Boulevard St. Michel for barricades, Parisians continued eating and drinking in cafés and restaurants close to the violence. In one favorite, La Méditerranée on the Place de l'Odéon, windows were broken but dinner was served with the whiff of tear gas flavoring the bouillabaisse, an exploded tear gas canister unnoticed on the floor.

In this enormous upheaval for France, there was no killing, while in the U.S. lethal violence continued. Robert Kennedy was assassinated in Los Angeles. That meant another dash to New York and another long funeral narration. It was followed it seemed in no time by the Chicago convention. The BBC rooms on the fifth floor in the Conrad Hilton Hotel put us directly above the police riot, as investigators later called it, in which Chicago policemen beat up students demonstrating for candidate Eugene McCarthy and against the war.

The observer of American character had to note the extraordinary variety on display that year. There was Hubert Humphrey, one of the last passionate believers in liberal solutions, a garrulous, inspiring orator of infectious sincerity, whom frustrated ambition had trapped like a hapless fly in LBJ's web.

There was his fellow senator from Minnesota, McCarthy, who challenged Johnson to stop the killing in Vietnam and toppled him—cool intellectual, aloof yet engaged, a poet's touch, and a talent for wounding insults.

There was the man he goaded into running, Robert Kennedy, who had been stealthily calibrating his opposition to LBJ until McCarthy forced the issue. Now the ruthless tactician turned idealist, promising a Kennedy restoration in a crusade for America's poor and hungry children.

There was Richard Nixon, skilled and farsighted in foreign affairs, paranoid and insecure at home, building a career on smears and dirty tricks, sanctimonious in public, vicious in private, willing, as we later learned, to break the law to stay in power. All this was American.

So were the decent people we visited in Iowa who formed that state's small delegation to the Republican convention. In Council Bluffs, Davenport, and Cedar Rapids, in backyards behind split-level houses, we had barbecue and iced tea and talked politics. These small-town bankers, insurance salesmen, agricultural machinery dealers were all earnestly devoted to Nixon. Only in Dubuque, at a handsome home on the Mississippi, were alcoholic drinks served—by the lone Rockefeller delegate.

And there was Spiro Agnew, the running mate Nixon employed as hatchet man against the press. When Agnew was chosen at the Miami convention, he agreed to an interview in my BBC room in the Eden Roc Hotel. We filmed him calling his son Randy on active service in Vietnam to tell him the good news. It made a nice way into the interview in which Agnew obligingly unburdened himself of views on several topics, including "law and order," then a campaign slogan. Agnew said that if a man was fleeing from the scene of a looting and would not stop, police were entitled to shoot him because "they did not know whether he was a looter, a rapist or whatever." There was a lot of such talk that year, but to hear such sentiments from a man trained in the law and likely to be vice president of the United States appalled me. The most notorious looters in 1968 were blacks enraged by the assassination of Martin Luther King, so there seemed to be sly appeals to racism in much of Agnew's rhetoric.

Watching politicians exploiting fear of violent crime fitted into an aspect of American political life I deplored. It produced increasingly punitive prison terms, effectively discarded rehabilitation of criminals, put more people behind bars than any other free country, and reinstituted the death penalty, which most developed countries had abandoned. It tolerated grossly inadequate defense counsel for poor black and Latino defendants disproportionately represented on death row, and dismissed any opposition as being "soft on crime"; all while promoting private gun ownership for the illusion of safety.

It has always been axiomatic to me that easy access to firearms inevitably makes robbery, fights, and private arguments more lethal. That view is widely held by police forces, criminologists, judges, and criminal psychiatrists. But that logic has made only creeping progress against the political forces for gun freedom. One of the last assignments I had for NBC News in 1967 had been a documentary entitled "Whose Right to Bear Arms." It exposed the hypocrisy of the National Rifle Association pretending to Congress to favor a measure of gun regulation, but telling its membership the opposite. After I had finished my work on the documentary, the NRA brought pressure through a tame congressman and the piece was reedited without my knowledge to allow the head of the NRA to filibuster and obscure the relevant point. It is easier to pander to the gun lobby than confront the reality, and no politics is free of panderers, even in the home of the brave. That continues to this day.

After the Miami convention, I drove several people up the coast to Palm Beach for dinner. Entering a town, I passed a car and, pulling back to the right, clipped a few yards of the double no-passing line. I was not speeding. Immediately a siren sounded and a police car with flashing lights pulled up behind. I pulled over and stopped, with the police car about twenty yards behind. I waited, expecting the cop to come up to my window. Instead I heard his loudspeaker, "Are you comin' out or am I comin' to get ya?" In the mirror I saw the patrolman standing by his car, legs apart, gun hand poised over his holster. So I got out and walked back to get out my (now British) driver's license and was given a ticket. I was stunned by the attitude of the cop and the culture of swaggering machismo he seemed to personify. I regarded police-men as public servants who owed nonthreatening people like me some basic courtesy. If they treat me so, how will they treat blacks or anyone lower on the socioeconomic scale than themselves? Ob-viously I was spoiled by the civility of the police I had dealt with in New York or Canada or Britain.

I wasn't keeping a running tally of pros and cons about U.S. society. But I did unconsciously tuck such issues into emotional pockets, as though I were holding America in a kind of probation. On this issue I thought Canada and Britain had a superior record. Perhaps I was subconsciously building a case to balance what was my growing fascination with America and pleasure in being part of it. Some part of me wanted to keep the options open.

America was a violent society compared with the others I knew, and its politicians and media often seemed to take that vio-lence for granted—an American tic or distinguishing characteris-tic, not a blot or a blight, but an immutable bit of the American DNA. Violence is a surefire ingredient in American entertainment, often presented as the acceptable solution to frustration, to being crossed, impeded in your mission; the cathartic resolution of per-sonal conflict, the essential measure of American manhood. The protypical American hero has evolved from the modest Gary Cooper or the ironic Bogart to Sylvester Stallone as Rambo. You cross him and you get wasted, blown to hell. Fine, it's all enter-tainment, good harmless fun. But it is a cultural value and it sends messages.

. . .

I was in the U.S. all that fall for the general election campaign and publication of my book, *The People Machine*, the first book on the influence of television on American politics, focusing on the huge amounts of money suddenly necessary as candidates surrendered to the new breed of media advisers and image-makers television campaigning demanded. The book was also, I believe, the first critique of network news, which intrigued a number of talk shows. On *The Merv Griffin Show*, I had the novelty of dictating the questions I was to be asked, and then watching Merv read them from a cue card over my shoulder. For the fledgling *Phil Donahue Show* in Dayton, Ohio, the publisher had scheduled a quick getaway by helicopter for another date. Donahue thought that showbizzy enough to invite his entire studio audience out into the parking lot to wave as the helicopter took off. Such publicity tempted me to think the book was destined for bestsellerdom but it wasn't. It was outshone by the inspired, novelistic reporting of Joe McGinnis in *The Selling of the President*. But my book was published in Britain and Japan, and it certainly annoyed some network news executives.

The book and my BBC reporting set me up to write and narrate a ninety-minute PBS special about television, "The Whole World Is Watching." That was what Czech protesters had chanted as Soviet tanks crushed the Prague Spring, and so had the McCarthy demonstrators in Chicago. Television had brought a new dimension to the worldwide turmoil of 1968. It was a vivid, usually objective witness, but inevitably it was a participant, at times a catalyst. In Chicago, videotape of police battles with antiwar demonstrators, shown by the networks during the convention proceedings, enraged establishment Democrats who were trying to lend some dignity to the preordained nomination of Vice President Humphrey. Television altered the way political reality was perceived—it created political theater.

As evidence of how Americo-centric I had become that summer, when I called London to protest about cuts in my Chicago film, the producer said, "Robin, Soviet tanks are in the streets of Prague as we speak." I had been so obsessed with U.S. politics I was oblivious to Prague, and to the civil war in Nigeria, which produced some of the most grisly television of the year.

Editing the Nigerian sequences for the documentary, I experienced an extraordinary moment of understanding of our medium and its arbitrary power. The scene showed a Nigerian army captain interrogating a Biafran rebel captive, who is almost naked, lying in the dust, hands and feet tied. Terrified, he keeps bleating, in English, "I am not a Biafran soldier! I am not a Biafran soldier! I am not a Biafran soldier!" his hysteria rising. The captain grabs a machine gun and riddles the captive, making his body leap and twitch on the road. On the editing machine we ran the film forward and back to find an edit point. At one moment, the captive was alive, then dead. Back and forth, you could find the exact frame where life left that pathetic body, reduced before our eyes to a black rag of empty flesh, then reawakens to a sentient being, begging for his life. It haunted me. What if the wife, or mother, of that wretched man could see this, pushing a lever to make him live and die and live? And how had television's very presence affected his fate?

Television gave the world many such moments that year.

. . .

In 1969, Jane and I bought our first house, a converted barn, dated 1483, half-timbered with herringbone brick, attached to an Elizabethan manor house in the village of Holyport, twenty miles west of London. With a mortgage guaranteed by the BBC, I felt we were planting ourselves in English soil as literally as I was the roses and fruit trees in our garden. At the end of the lane was the village green with a pub I liked. London Airport was fifteen minutes away, the BBC half an hour, central London fifteen minutes more. Our growing band of friends came out from London for dinner and brought children on weekends. We had dances with a steel band. Our children were in challenging schools. My work was always absorbing. America was a place to go for stories, often in those years stories suggesting a dislocated society, as when National Guard troops fired on student protesters at Kent State University.

Otherwise, I covered more British politics, Britain's flirtation with the advancing European Common Market, the crisis in Italian communism after Prague. The last meant two weeks in the ancient city of Bologna and a nearby village. The backbone of our report was the struggle between the village priest and the fat little communist mayor, straight from the delightful Don Camillo novels of Giovanni Guareschi.

The glory of my base in London, with the world to cover, was that we were frequently shooting off to places tourists yearned to go. You worked hard, sometimes impossibly long hours, but all the while you were eating and sleeping and learning about that piece of the world as few tourists can. Two weeks in Bologna, one of the great restaurant cities of Europe, where merely to be polite to one's sources required curiosity about the local food and wine. I loved the travel, as I loved the craft of quick documentary reportage, the combination of creative filmmaking and journalism, which the BBC's technical standards brought to a high level. Professionally, I believed I was a happy man.

I was so convinced that we would be permanently based in

London that when we spent a month in a Portuguese village on the Algarve in the summer of 1971, we bought very cheaply a fisherman's stone house with the idea of renovating it. It was in a village well away from the fashionable end of the Algarve, surrounded by fig trees and pomegranates, amid groves of olive and almond trees. The nearby town of Tavira had fresh fish, fruit and vegetable markets, the local wine was about fifty cents a gallon, and half an hour away was Faro airport with direct flights from London. I hired a local gardener to plant grapevines and fruit trees in front of the house, with a little system for irrigation. More roots. But I got distracted and he used the nicely watered soil to grow his garlics, ignoring my vines.

Back home in Britain that fall, I got a call from Jim Karayn, a producer I had worked with in Washington who was setting up a kind of putative news department for public television. Would I come for a year to cover the 1972 election as a senior correspondent with Sandy Vanocur, for what I had earned my last year at NBC? Since that was three times what I was making at the BBC, I figured that I could do Washington for a year, cover the lower American taxes, plus some arrears in British taxes, and pay for the new kitchen we'd installed. That was the rationale. The BBC graciously gave me a leave of absence, we rented the Holyport house, and moved to Washington. Now I am amazed when I remember now how casually, unpremeditatedly, these important turning points were decided.

9

THE NORTH AMERICAN

I was switching once again from the Canadian guy who'd been telling Brits about the Americans, to telling Americans about themselves. Each time I had to switch attitudes, not just spelling the word *program* "programme" in BBC scripts, but putting myself into the minds of the British, or Americans, or Canadians: their assumptions about themselves, their knowledge, their level of disinterest or curiosity about the world outside. I needed to know what concepts excited their patriotism and xenophobia.

I have always imagined one sympathetic reader or viewer or listener who understood me. But in each country I had to reach for him or her differently, like tuning to a different frequency, to imagine whom I was addressing. Again the outsider, inevitably a little drier-eyed than the natives in certain rituals, although the longer I spent in each country, the warmer my empathy.

The tension between the emotional coolness Canadians of my background tended to exhibit, and the tug on the heartstrings that comes from sharing another people's heartbreaks, created my journalistic persona. It was always in flux, since my focus kept shifting, each shift creating another layer of experience and, probably, modifying the persona. My apparent coldness (I wish I could claim cool) led an early reviewer of our efforts in Washington to call Vanocur and me "the balding hippie and his icy blond sidekick."

One year's leave from the BBC became two, and momentous years they were. Sandy and I covered the 1972 presidential election with a series of quite original and unbiased weekly reports. But from the start we were besieged by a calculated campaign in the Nixon White House to undermine us within the public television community. Documents later obtained by the Carnegie Commission show President Nixon and his staff plotting to threaten public television stations with loss of their federal funding if they carried our programs. Since public broadcasters were already uneasy about adding journalism to their cultural and educational fare, the threat was potent. The administration also leaked our salaries, angering some congressmen who were paid less. In effect, they tried to smother the infant PBS news effort in its cradle. We survived and thrived, ironically, on the downfall of Richard Nixon.

It happened like this: Sandy left after a year of being a lightning rod, and his place was taken by Jim Lehrer, a newspaperman from Texas who quickly became my close friend. Within a few months we found ourselves anchoring the Senate hearings on Watergate. Public Television carried the hearings live and repeated them in the evenings. Ratings and donations to PBS stations shot up, qualms about being in the news business were stilled. After forty-seven days and nights of hearings, people began to suggest that Jim and I do a nightly news program. We were willing, but could not persuade management that he and I should be the editors as well as the on-air anchors. We were determined to call our own tune: we'd had enough of jumping through the silly hoops some producers devised.

The craziest I experienced was for a program on changes in tort law and a profile of Melvin Belli, the colorful San Francisco attorney who provoked those changes.

To introduce my interview with Belli, the producer had me drive repeatedly across the Golden Gate Bridge in a convertible, talking to a camera located in a helicopter whizzing alongside the bridge. To get the timing right we did so many takes that a police helicopter finally came and chased us away. The sequence continued in Belli's Telegraph Hill apartment. Speaking to camera, I walked through his living room and out to a balcony, concluding to the camera in the helicopter now hovering outside. Unhappily, the downdraft from its rotors blew away the spring flowers from all the little terraced gardens down the hill. Police again . . . damages to garden owners . . . great PR for public TV!

That was part of a series anchored from the studio, which required Jim and me to walk so many paces, stop at a motorized ball that revolved as a superimposed videotape flashed onto it, deliver a paragraph of script, walk to another ball and do the same. Neither the balls, nor we, nor the videotape ever quite coincided, necessitating many retakes. At 2:30 one morning, after seventeen takes, I said flatly, No more takes.

Lehrer and I were adamant never again to submit to such foolishness in the name of "production values" that had nothing to do with journalism. But the management types insisted we could not be on air and editors. We fought all the summer of 1973 as I wavered whether to stay or go back to my job in England—or to Canada.

In Toronto, Bill Cunningham, an old friend, was just starting a news division for Global Television, a new commercial network, and wanted me to anchor his nightly news. Thus all my allegiances—British, American, and Canadian—were tugging at me. For the first time since I had left in 1955, I was really tempted to return.

Canada was undergoing a cultural revolution. A wave of multicultural immigration was changing the national complexion, eating habits, and mores, loosening the moral straitjacket of the Anglo-Scottish primacy I had grown up with. The new politics that arrived in the late '60s with Pierre Trudeau's dashing persona were, as far as government could, relaxing an uptight and censorious society. As justice minister, Trudeau had liberalized grounds for divorce and decriminalized many acts, including homosexuality between consenting adults in private. Trudeau became famous for saying, "The state has no place in the nation's bedroom."

Since 1965 and the NBC documentary on Quebec nationalism, I had paid little attention to Canada. There always seemed to be bigger stories elsewhere so, even though I visited my mother and brothers, I was a relative stranger in my native country.

That began to change in 1970, when Quebec terrorists kidnapped a British diplomat and a provincial cabinet minister, Pierre Laporte, whom they strangled with the chain of his Catholic medal and stabbed to death with an ice pick. Trudeau, now prime minister, invoked the War Measures Act, mobilizing the armed forces and suspending civil liberties. The story broke the day our son William was born in London, and the next day I left for Canada to report for the BBC. In Ottawa, I called on a childhood friend, Don Macdonald, who was now Trudeau's minister of justice. He lived in a leafy suburb, the house set back behind tall trees. As my car stopped, a soldier in full battle gear materialized from behind each tree, brandishing a machine gun. A totally incongruous sight in the capital, where the most violent happening was the extreme cold in winter. Since news follows violence, Canada was suddenly on everyone's map.

On the way back to London to edit the piece, I wrote, as I often did, a story about the experience for the BBC magazine, *The Listener*. When it appeared, I got an approving letter from the Canadian writer Mordecai Richler, who lived in London. Reading his novels, I felt some revived curiosity about Canada.

In 1972, to considerable publicity, Richler returned to his native Montreal. In some circles that was seen as a confirmation that Canada was now a magnet that attracted, and no longer repelled, its young talent.

By then lots of serious writers were brightening the Canadian literary scene, but I felt a special affinity for Richler. His novels explored Canadian identity with a bawdy, hilarious irreverence. He made the richer ethnic and religious variety of Canada impossible to ignore, giving Canadians a larger sense of themselves, casting a merciless eye not just on his Jewish roots but on everyone, deconstructing all our myths.

So what had seemed a cultural desert in the 1950s had begun to bloom as a wave of creative confidence swept through theater, literature and publishing, music, filmmaking, and dance. It was exciting; Canada was at last hearing its own voice, and it made Toronto seem a truly attractive option.

In the end, however, the pull of the familiar was too strong. I opted for London, the BBC job, the house, the schools, the friends in England, gratefully leaving behind the rancors of Washington public television. Although as an institution it had just won enormous vindication with Watergate, public broadcasting continued to suffer from dissension and self-doubt. If I was going to stay committed to noncommercial television, the obvious place was where it flowered most fruitfully, and that was the BBC.

Now I was back talking not to Americans but to the British, though often about American events. The threatened impeachment and subsequent resignation of Richard Nixon and the accession of Gerald Ford kept me flying back to Washington. There I would immerse myself in a new development, interview as many key players as possible, dash for Dulles Airport, spend the night on the TWA direct flight organizing notes and making a cutting order, then go straight to the editing rooms at the BBC's Lime Grove Studios and virtually live there until the film was cut, dubbed, and ready for air at 8 P.M. Monday.

The climax of Watergate offered me another vivid lesson in American character: there was the doughty, drawling, small-town southern judge, Sam Ervin, the canny Democrat who chaired the Senate hearings. Beside him for the Republicans was Howard Baker, the Tennessee senator whose judicious evenhandedness surmounted his partisan loyalties. There was the tortured attorney general, Elliot Richardson, who resigned rather than shield Nixon. There were the House Republicans such as William Cohen who voted for impeachment. Suddenly, integrity and political courage were carrying the day. It was inspiring. And the man who replaced Nixon, Gerald Ford, stolidly impervious to media ridicule by force of his uncomplicated and wholesome demeanor, calmed the nation, even if he infuriated many by pardoning Nixon. How could I not admire a nation that produced such character in order to drag itself out of such a mess?

My Nixon coverage had an interesting sequel. Partly at my urging, the BBC decided to devote an evening to the rise and fall of this man, this tragicomedy of the television age, all his crises so minutely documented on the medium of the era. I drafted an outline for a documentary drama. The man who ran BBC 1, Aubrey Singer, was intrigued but thought we needed a long interview with Nixon on which to build the rest. A hopeless quest, I thought. Nixon, in seclusion at San Clemente, was speaking to no one. Still, I composed a careful letter to him with a rationale for why he might wish to use the BBC to break his silence. I leaned heavily on my early good relations with him and my determination to be fair, ignoring his assaults on us at PBS. With the letter I flew to Los Angeles, where a friend gave me a phone number for Nixon's loyal aide, Marine lieutenant colonel Jack Brennan, whom the nation had last seen defiantly barking, "The President of the United States" as Nixon left the White House for good. Colonel Brennan agreed to accept the letter and I drove to Casa Pacifica off the San Diego Freeway. The house was hidden by eucalyptus trees. I came to a metal gate and stopped the car. There was a whirring sound and the gatepost extruded a combination microphone-speaker and a voice asked what I wanted. When I explained, it said, "Wait there!" A few minutes later a Secret Service man appeared in a car and took the envelope.

Not daring to leave the phone, I waited for five days in the Beverly Wilshire Hotel, trying to work on a novel but too distracted. Then Colonel Brennan called to say that Mr. Nixon was "quite interested" in our proposal and put me in touch with his agent, Irving Lazar in New York, who had sold Nixon's memoirs for $2 million. "Swifty" Lazar was easy to reach and very direct. They would give me, on a world exclusive basis, four or five one-hour interviews with the former president for $1 million.

Amazed, I flew back to London rationalizing that, with leeway to negotiate a lower price, the interviews could be sold to many countries and would in the end cost the BBC nothing.

But Aubrey Singer declared he was not going to pay "a pardoned felon a million dollars for his memoirs." Eventually his business sense overcame that scruple; after I left the BBC in 1975, David Frost did the interviews for $600,000.

. . .

My last years with the BBC offered a great variety of assignments.

I did a one-hour profile of Rose Kennedy, which involved long interviews at her houses in Palm Beach and Hyannis overlooking the lawn and beach grass, where years before on summer weekends I had been brought in with other reporters to witness the president's arrival by helicopter.

I got a rare backstage look at this indomitable woman. We were setting up the camera and lights in the living room at Hyannis when a voice called from upstairs, "Where's the one who's going to ask the questions?" I went up to find Mrs. Kennedy sitting in her bedroom facing a wall of mirrored closets as a makeup man began his labors. She was wearing a white slip, an old housecoat, and black lace-up shoes, nun's shoes. The makeup man was just applying a false eyelash.

"Is this the one who will be asking the questions?" she asked without turning. Her secretary introduced me. Mrs. Kennedy gave me no salutation but said, "I have dictated what I want to say in the interview. It's been typed up. You'll find it there on the bed. Bring it over and sit down and we'll go through it."

I retrieved the typescript from the four-poster bed. Lying there was the new blue Cardin wool dress to be worn for the first time in our interview.

I sat on a small stool she indicated beside her, feeling like the man brought upstairs to polish her shoes. I spent an hour talking her out of delivering prepared rhapsodies about Queen Elizabeth, the Queen Mother, and the like while the makeup man transformed her from a woman of eighty-three with large age freckles to someone who, if you squinted, might have passed for forty. Downstairs, when she settled herself in a wing chair, the lights came on, the camera rolled, and she lifted the heavy eyelashes to reveal hyacinth blue eyes the color of her dress, the effect was stunning, a great actress taking the stage.

As I got her to address the tragedies in her life, it was clear she identified both with the burdens of queenship and the torments of the Virgin Mary.

"I think I've had great tragedies, and I think of the Blessed Mother when she watched her son being crucified and reviled, and she still trusted in God and she bore everything patiently; and I thought of her so often at the Crucifixion when I saw Jack [lying in state] in Washington, and Bobby again in New York."

Her voice faltered and I thought she was going to break down but she quickly stiffened her back, cocked her head defiantly on one side, and laughed: "And I'm not going to be vanquished either—so I'm going to carry on. I think God intends us to be happy. We must live for the living."

And so she did—for two more decades.

Because of that program, the family asked me to host a celebration for Rose's one-hundredth birthday. So I found myself in those houses in Hyannis, drinking cocktails and eating meals in spurious intimacy with surviving Kennedys of several generations—all of whom, like the rest of the world, I knew only from a distance.

For *Panorama* I did three one-hour programs on the experience of Pakistani immigrants living in England, winning extraordinary access to a young Muslim wife wrenched out of the supportive embrace of a large extended family on a Punjabi farm and installed alone in a small damp cold house in a grim street in the north of England. One of the hours we shot around her home village in Pakistan, which involved living for a month the rhythms of rural Muslim life, awakening to the call of the muezzin in the nearby mosque, drinking milky tea cooked over a sweet-smelling fire of dried dung; and being shown the subtle meanings in various adjustments of women's veils.

That series had an obvious corollary, a documentary profile of Enoch Powell, the Conservative politician who was fanning racial tensions by campaigning against further Pakistani and other non-white immigration. Powell had a touch of fanaticism, a hypnotic stare and Hitlerish mustache that could give an uncharitable observer nasty associations. By extraordinary self-discipline he had risen from humble origins to become a classics scholar, then a public figure.

I was intrigued by him and, in a dim, semiconscious way, hurt by how easily Britain, so tolerant a society, embraced racist expediency and simply rescinded the long-held rights of citizens of its former colonies. In changing its citizenship laws, even some British passports (like those held by Hong Kong residents) became invalid for migration to Britain. While most British politicians disavowed it, Enoch Powell's alarmist rhetoric had its effect.

Powell's condescending manner irritated me. In a long interview, I asked how he *envisaged* something or other. Schoolmasterishly, Powell corrected me, "You don't mean *envisage*, you mean *envision*." I said I meant *envisage*, literally to put a face on something, to imagine it. Oh no, he said smugly, "*Envision. Envisage* shows your colonial background." But later, checking the full *Oxford English Dictionary*, I found *envisage* meant precisely what I'd intended, "to obtain a mental view of, to set before the mind's eye," from the French *envisager. Envision*, curiously enough, was not given in the first edition, but snuck in more recently.

Years later I was amused to receive a book entitled *The State of the Language* and find articles by me and Powell next to each other. His was a complaint about lapses in grammar, typically prescriptivist; mine a passage from my memoir *Wordstruck* about childhood and language and decidedly descriptivist. That was a stance I had found congenial while helping to make the television series *The Story of English* for the BBC and PBS.

My exchange with Powell ended up on the cutting room floor but his remark had touched a nerve: the cultural insecurity of the British colonial. Obviously some of my satisfaction in succeeding at the BBC, that most British institution, was the credential it gave the arrived colonial in me. Nothing would have pried such an admission from me then. But Powell's needle pricked open the conviction that I was North American. I found it hard to explain this late-blooming epiphany to my British friends. I remember many sessions where I tried to make sense of it. As a Cockney might say, "It just came all over me, like." I had never been under any illusion about being British, or English. The moment I set foot in England, my youthful fantasies had popped like a soap bubble. Or had they merely evaporated into my unconscious, only now surfacing to be faced and finally stared down? As I have said, I was quite content to be the Canadian who lived in England. Some people at the BBC wondered whether their audience would object to my accent, but I never heard that anyone did, until, significantly, they heard me a decade later narrating the nine hours of *The Story of English*.

That choice had been discussed beforehand. I had suggested, if the BBC thought it sensitive, that they have an English voice narrate the British version. The program logic, however, was that English was now the world language, and that North American usage was not only hugely influential but, since World War II, driving the language worldwide. English was no longer Britain's language only, and having a North American voice, albeit a somewhat mid-Atlantic one, tell the story, seemed appropriate. A few British viewers did protest about this non-English voice telling them about *their* language. The series was a success in many countries—Australian Broadcasting ran it twice, back to back, PBS ran it four times—but was less successful in England.

So, what was the meaning of this sudden conviction that I was *North American*? I had rejected the job in America and the offer in Canada and come back to Britain where the work was totally congenial ... but I now knew that Britain wasn't my country. I couldn't find *my country* in Britain. It was disconcerting, to awaken from all that childhood conditioning, all my yearnings. I was dazed, in some awe, puzzled about why this had crept over me now ... at the age of forty-four. I think it meant that I had needed to experience my own personal decolonization, living it out among the British. Having accomplished that, I suddenly felt stifled there.

With the British pay scale, taxes, and cost of living, it seemed impossible to get ahead of the game financially, and that desire was more North American than British. I was the father of four with no savings, a contract employee with no pension plan, and life insurance that covered only the house mortgage.

An advertising agency called from New York one evening, asking if I would do commercials for a painkilling drug that would present me in a news anchor format. The money promised was huge. I fantasized for a few hours and then called to refuse. I couldn't do commercials and remain a journalist.

As usual, there were other reasons. These turning points were never wholly rational; there were always too many emotional factors involved. My marriage with Jane had become very rocky, at times mutually insupportable, and close to crashing.

Magazines just then were full of stories about male menopause. I noted the symptoms, physical and psychological, that popular journalism listed, and one in particular resonated. Men of that age begin to fear competition from younger men. I could feel it, tiny jealousies arising when someone younger was praised or given a plum assignment—ridiculous on the surface because I had plenty of recognition and my choice of assignments. I would feel vaguely at risk, without being able to put my finger on it. The gradualness of this self-discovery was boring my friends and mystifying me. And then the fog cleared a little. If I were to insulate myself from competitive young talent, the best way would be to harness it: therefore, I needed to run something myself. That opportunity, as it happened, was being offered by friends in New York.

Ever since I had left Washington, convinced a nightly news program on PBS was impossible given the politics, WNET/Channel 13 in New York had been suggesting that Jim Lehrer and I do it there. I had been saying (and believing) no, I was happy at the BBC and didn't want to reenter that paranoid world of American public television—the backbiting, chronic underfunding, and political timidity.

For two years WNET kept working on me. Robert Kotlowitz, novelist and former editor at *Harper's* magazine, was head of programming, the man responsible for originating much of the national schedule that was defining PBS, including *Nature, Live from Lincoln Center, Great Performances*, and *Dance in America*. Kotlowitz stopped by whenever he was in Europe, and as our friendship grew, my resistance weakened. He said I could have carte blanche to design a news program, no difficulty about being on the air and the editor. I could team up with Lehrer, whom I'd been keeping informed on my frequent trips to Washington. It was tantalizing. A freer hand than anyone had ever offered me. A chance to put my ideas about a more serious use of television into practice. But very risky. To move my whole family back to the U.S. once again; give up whatever security we had—job, house, schools—to launch a new progam that could fizzle in a week?

When I had first left the BBC on the leave of absence, Huw Weldon, the managing director of television, a twinkling and garrulous Welshman, had Jane and me to lunch to convince us to make the absence temporary. After lunch he led us on a two-hour intimate tour of the Television Centre, the vast facilities for drama—wardrobe and costume shops, makeup, wig department, scenery design and construction. It was like Hollywood in the heyday of the major studios. He left us saying, "You'll never see anything like this in America."

Weldon frequently said, "There is only one way to make good

television. Some chap comes to you with a good idea, he has a good record, you ask him, How much? He says, Two million pounds. You give him the money and he makes the series. It may be rubbish, but the chances are it won't be. That's how to make good television."

When I told Kotlowitz the story, he said that he and John Jay Iselin, president of Channel 13, were proposing just that—$1.4 million dollars they had set aside that we could spend as we saw fit.

It was a funny argument that finally tipped my scales. Kotlowitz said, "Let me tell you what David Halberstam says about Jay Iselin: he's a man who doesn't leave his wounded on the battlefield."

And so I went to New York for such a tangle of motives that I couldn't have anaylzed them. The last thing on my mind was nationality, although we had to retrieve Will's passport from the U.S. embassy.

10

THE MACNEIL–LEHRER NEWSHOUR

think it was the fact of being an outsider that gave me the detachment to try something really different. Part of that was the Canadian sensibility, nurtured from childhood by the CBC's public service broadcasting ethic, later reinforced by my admiration for the BBC.

From all the years I had been running around the world for various news organizations, one story seemed to symbolize what disenchanted me about television news.

In September 1962 a Super Constellation plane (four-engine, propeller driven) of Flying Tiger Airlines had to ditch at night in the Atlantic six hundred miles west of Ireland. It was carrying U.S. servicemen and their wives back to Europe. With superb handling and discipline, fifty-one of the sixty people on board got out into life rafts. Three died of exposure, leaving forty-eight survivors on the ocean. Ships and planes of many nations joined the rescue effort, and journalists from all over Europe descended on Shannon, Ireland. I went there for NBC with cameraman Chris Callery and soundman Digby Jones.

Four survivors were brought ashore first and we recorded their moving stories. A larger group was aboard a freighter bound for Antwerp. While we waited, Chris and I had been promising ourselves a dinner of the renowned Shannon estuary lobster. The lobsters arrived just as Digby Jones rushed in. He was a generation older than us, a type the British call a "boffin," or mad scientist, with disheveled hair, spectacles mended with electrical tape. Interviewing James Thurber a few months earlier, I had introduced Digby and Thurber had said, "A *sound* man, how rare it is to meet one!"

Digby's hobby was listening to shortwave radio, and he had just picked up an emergency signal from the freighter. There had been a fire on board, with several people injured. The Irish Coast Guard had arranged a rendezvous for the following morning at 8 A.M., ten miles due south of Cork.

We glanced around the restaurant where many of our competitors were dining and realized that we could scoop them all! Leaving the lobsters untouched, we slunk out, got the camera, gear, and raced through the night to Cork.

On the narrow, twisting roads, we kept losing our way. In one village we stopped to ask directions from the Gàrda, the Irish police, and I stumbled on a curb, twisting my ankle badly. They helped me into the police station. The Gàrda officer gave me a swig of John Powers whiskey, then bound up my ankle using the elastic bandage off Digby's varicose veins.

On painfully to Cork, arriving just after dawn. We found a fisherman willing to take us out and were breaking off to have breakfast when he said, Oh no, we had to leave immediately.

With ill grace we humped the gear into his open boat and proceeded out of the harbor. Soon the swells increased, the wind blew spray in our faces, and our growling stomachs began to feel decidedly queasy. The fisherman cheerfully offered us swigs of his poteen, the illicit spirit distilled from potatoes.

After two hours he announced that we were ten miles out due south of Cork. As the seas lifted us, we scanned the horizon: no sign of any ship or helicopter. We waited an hour, wallowing in that sea, furious at ourselves for being so foolish. Then we turned back in, taking two hours more.

We landed and I dragged my throbbing ankle up the tide-exposed ladder, planning to cut our losses with a good lunch. But we turned on the car radio to hear that the survivors were about to be landed at a hospital in Kinsale, twelve miles away. Damn it! We drove like madmen through the narrow lanes and arrived, miraculously, the moment the survivors did. With other television crews we set up our camera and recorded the stories, one of which I will never forget.

A U.S. Army captain had survived but his wife had been lost. With tears in his eyes he described the moments as the plane ditched:

"We were catapulted forward in a bunch. The safety belts held but the seats broke loose. It was pitch dark and the water was pouring in. I didn't see my wife again after that." The captain faltered, tried to regain control, then broke down and wept. All you could hear were his sobs and the whirring of the 16mm cameras.

We packed up to race back to Shannon to ship our film to

New York. In the lobby we passed the grieving captain. A British TV reporter was pleading with him, "I'm terribly sorry but I was late. Would you mind awfully just doing that bit again?"

The captain looked at him haggardly, "What bit?"

"The bit where you tell about your wife and then break down."

The captain turned contemptuously away. In the car, I thanked God I wasn't that reporter forced to be so callous because he didn't have "the bit" that everyone would carry that night, the bit producers would jump on and run again and again in each newscast, the bit without which the TV reporter is lost.

In most stories television cared to cover there was always the right bit—the most violent, most bloody, most pathetic, tragic, heartwarming, awful moment. Getting that bit was effectively what television news was all about.

Now I was convinced that there must be another way. There should be one place on television where things could be slowed down, where a quiet, more thoughtful treatment of the daily news would be possible. And from these ruminations, and Jim Lehrer's matching philosophy, came the program that rapidly became an institution.

After two months of preparation we went on the air in October 1975 with a simple alternative to network news, broadcast at WNET's inspiration in the half hour following them. We called it a complement to them, in which we analyzed one story for thirty minutes, with up to four guests offering differing views.

Some weeks before, WNET's publicity director, Angela Solomon, asked what we were going to call the program. I got out a pad with names I had been playing with, whiz-bang names like *Newsbeat, Newsnight, Newswatch*—all sounding like something already on the air. This savvy New Yorker looked at me sardonically and said, "I thought we had hired somebody smart."

"What do you mean?"

"The most distinctive title you can use is your own name."

"But," said the ingenuous Canadian, "what if a year from now Channel 13 isn't happy? They may want to put in someone instead of me."

"Dummy!" she said.

Because of Angela Solomon, and because it originated in New York, our program at first was called *The Robert MacNeil Report*, with Jim Lehrer reporting from Washington. It was soon distributed nationally by PBS, and by the following spring, with the Washington station WETA now a coproducer, it became *The MacNeil-Lehrer Report*.

Our format and editorial treatment ran against the grain of television at the time, which despised what producers called the "talking head." We not only resurrected it but gloried in it, convinced that the talking head was the still the most vital form of human communication, and made the face on the TV screen close to life-size. We extracted full visual value from our conversations, shooting them in the round, guests gathered at a horseshoe desk. Originating from two cities, we played that up, with a nod to *The Huntley-Brinkley Report*, alternating interviews between New York and Washington, creating variety and movement.

We stressed coherence and editorial discipline. We inverted the usual pyramid of television economy (production values dominating editorial), with beat reporters heavily outnumbering producers. And we stressed fairness.

I had thought I was a fair-minded person until I ran into Jim Lehrer, whose anger at sloppy, careless, or self-important journalism exceeds even mine. A quality I have never encountered in such pure form is Lehrer's moral clarity. Whatever the issue, a story to be parsed, a staff problem, or personal difficulty, he sees the ethical equation just about instantly. And yet he is no moralizer; he has a fresh and wicked sense of humor that meshes well with mine. Finally, he has enough imagination for all of us. He teems with new ideas, so many ideas that he never needs to hold any too jealously. The only differences we have had, I see now, usually arose from his solid Americanism and my gradual and grudging progress toward that.

Our program caught on because it was original and it answered a real journalistic need. There was nothing like it on television at a time when most cities had a maximum of three network channels, perhaps one independent, and an educational, or public station. We created a new journalistic form. By letting the audience eavesdrop as we debriefed the best news sources we could assemble, viewers became, in effect, reporters themselves. In their own minds they separated what sources were saying into fact, opinion, propaganda. And the viewers made the synthesis. They, not we, figured out what it meant. We weren't telling them what to think, we were encouraging them to think. It was a new dynamic and it quickly became popular among news addicts. Some viewers followed our ads that suggested they watch Walter Cronkite, then watch us.

We had our disasters. Committed to half an hour for one story of live television meant we had no parachute if things went wrong, as they did. Intrigued by a *New Yorker* article about tomatoes being bred to withstand rough shipping (with impact resistance relatively greater than the EPA required for car bumpers) we devoted a program to "The Square Tomato" as a symbol of where America was going if consumers demanded seasonal products all year round. To be fair, we bought tomatoes at random and opened the program with a tomato expert cutting into them on the desk in front of me. The first cut released the delicious perfume of perfect tomato, so did the next and the next. We had to talk for half an hour about lousy tomatoes corrupting the culture, and all the examples we had were perfect.

We were told that we should be alarmed about the rapid depletion of the water table because development and agriculture were pushing rapidly into drier parts of the country. We focused on the Ogallala Aquifer, whose water level was dropping by a foot a year and being replenished by only one inch a year. Disaster loomed, but how urgently? I asked the first guest, the most alarmed of our sources, when would it become critical. Oh, he said casually, about the year 2030. Try keeping that vital for thirty minutes—in 1976.

The third night on the air we discussed Spain after Franco. Franco, inconsiderately, took another month to die.

Still, the audience forgave us our gaffes, the program grew more popular, more public stations carried it, and corporate underwriters appeared.

The program infinitely deepened my understanding of America. I lived total immersion in American life and values, issues and personalities. There was the obvious professional level: the stories we covered, the preparation needed and sources used, the people we interviewed, from presidents to welfare mothers. Added to that was my daily personal experience of our staff, carefully chosen to create a congenial working environment, free as we could make it of the sadistic and hypercompetitive culture that exists elsewhere on television. So my colleagues became another family—an

American family—and through them I shared intimately in the psychological minutiae of American attitudes, opening the human reality of America to me more personally than ever before. Some became friends so trusted I shared everything with them.

Subtly, my reservations about the United States were being eroded, my sharper attitudes pumiced away, weathered down by the fine winds and rains of everyday experience; a process ridiculously gradual—a geological pace, I suppose—a process by which I exchanged defensive abstractions for human reality. These people thought and felt as I did about public issues, private morality, whatever. They found absurd what I found absurd about America, admirable what I did, funny what I laughed at, and despised what I despised. And gradually it came into my consciousness that there must be millions of Americans—more perhaps than the population of Canada—who felt as I did, when the *they* of opinion polls became the *we* of shared American experience.

Ariel Dorfman, the Chilean writer said, "You become part of the country that you're living in, because if you don't, you will live in a double exile." *Double exile* resonated. I believe for a time I had been defensively cultivating that creature, the exiled me, feathering its nest, keeping it warm . . . in case of need to escape.

. . .

If New York City rapidly became as congenial as London, the community where we lived did not. We first rented and later bought in Bronxville, a Westchester suburb.

I am not a suburban creature, preferring big cities or deep country. The suburban compromise unsettles me, as Bronxville did, particularly with its complacency, its lily-white (save for a few

Japanese) school system, and its anti-Semitism, half an hour from New York, the largest Jewish city in the world with a culture that owes much of its vibrancy to Jews. We went to dinner one evening where the hosts boasted at length of how they had prevented a Jewish couple from buying a house next door. There were Jews living in Bronxville. One of them, an eminent surgeon, was a fellow guest that evening, listening impassively to this harangue.

The primary school hired a new principal, a woman probably too pretty to put the community matrons at ease. At Christmas she taught the children a few Hanukkah songs in addition to the Christian carols. Word of this dangerous multiculturalism flashed around the telephones of Bronxville and, getting the message, she resigned. Many in Bronxville deplored such attitudes, including Jane, but the overall climate made me feel I did not belong there. That contributed to the many other difficulties in our marriage. In 1981 we separated and I moved into Manhattan.

. . .

Living in New York, not across the Atlantic, let me visit my family more often and cover Canadian stories.

The 1976 election for a new government in Quebec attracted wide attention because of the challenge mounted by the Parti Québécois, promising to take Quebec out of Canada. With *The MacNeil-Lehrer Report* now established and gaining confidence, we went to Montreal to cover the election that could transform Canada—and did. The PQ won, making its charismatic leader, the chain-smoking former journalist René Lévesque, the premier. Seeking an interview, I got nowhere with his delirious staff, but I did get there—through my uncle, Corty.

I was born on the English side of the Two Solitudes at a time when the metaphorical title of Hugh MacLennan's celebrated novel was cruel fact. My grandmother's house, which we often visited, was only six doors away from Pierre Elliott Trudeau's childhood home. But more than age (he was eleven years older) divided us. There was never the slightest chance of our meeting. At our end of McCulloch Avenue in Outremont, there was no social contact between French and English Canadians.

When I was a boy in the 1940s, my father's talented brother Corty, an actor and a good mimic, had a routine imitating a French radio baseball commentator screaming: "Louis Batisse frappe la balle. La balle est en extérieur!" [Louis Batisse gets a hit. It's a home run!] Hilarious: he'd have us in tears. Yet in 1976 it was the same Uncle Corty, an advertising executive with Bell Telephone, who got me through the thickets of rapturous separatists to an exclusive interview with Lévesque.

Unlike thousands of "Anglos" who fled as Quebec nationalism grew more extreme, Corty had outgrown his prejudice and embraced the other culture of his city. He learned idiomatic Montreal French and used it with political cronies in the taverns.

· · ·

Visiting Canada more often, the first emotion I noticed was a little thrill in actually going north. A sense of the North is bred in Canadians. It defines Canada as the presence of the U.S. defines it to the south. Canadians are ambivalent about the North: it causes them to expend so much energy and ingenuity to make life comfortable, yet appropriating the North, dealing with it, is a source of pride and helps define the Canadian character.

I feel it looking at the landscape painters from the early twentieth century, known to all Canadians from mass reproductions. Before and after World War I, which some of them painted in the trenches, these painters turned their backs on the world, seeking Canada's difference. To look east was to look back to Europe and the horrors they had just seen. To look south was to see the United States. North was the way they turned to face their own distinctiveness.

In many pictures by Tom Thomson, A. Y. Jackson, and Lawren Harris, there is a loneliness (they seldom depict people), yet a pleasure in loneliness, as though the mystery of the North were pulling you deeper into it. Even when the colors in the foreground are cheerful, they are chilled by the dark horizons beyond—purple, slate gray—heavy skies marching endlessly northward. These painters felt it in the late afternoon light when the sky chills, the world seems to go out, the little warmth of the shorter days near the solstice steals down over the curve of the earth, and the primordial chill returns. A northern feeling, that the light was going to fail—the most primitive fear of man. In that wilderness when the light fails, you are not as confident as you are farther south that it will be relumed the next morning.

Yet there is a contrary emotion, daring you to live there, to admire it, not to be content to live only where life is easy. With that is another Canadian feeling, the welcoming, protective feel of the woods in wintertime, as rich in resources to sustain life as in threats to it.

Now also, in my late forties, I returned more often to Nova Scotia, my childhood home, finding magic in what had bored me at twenty-one. I felt a richness of emotion in childhood memories that would surprise no psychologist, and I realized that those feelings had informed the experiences I'd been having in all the other places. Memory is not just about the past; it continues to inform and alter the present.

I found Halifax and the nearer parts of Nova Scotia rich in mystery for me. I began recalling smells—the mud in the schoolyard in spring, birch catkins squashed into the sidewalk. Why was that sensual memory so strong? What other memory was it the key to? And what part did that emotion play in the construction of the man who remembered it now and sensed some clue there? Halifax was so full of clues that it had become the doorway to my imagination. In fact, going back to Nova Scotia enabled me finally to become the writer I had been trying to be for three decades.

That also made me desire to have a place of my own in Nova Scotia and so I began to use visits to my family to look.

Yet I would always feel that returning to New York was coming home, to my city, my workplace, and most of my friends. And I was entirely satisfied professionally.

In 1983 our program expanded into *The MacNeil-Lehrer NewsHour*, the first full hour of evening news on American television, a real alternative to the commercial network news, and it was growing in influence. I had no incentive to leave New York.

The expanded program and budget gave us the resources to broaden our reach, to give the hour variety of texture. It became the only daily news program to offer extended documentary reports and coverage of hearings, news conferences, and speeches fuller in context than the brief clips on the commercial news. The program went to political conventions; it covered elections and debates. In fact, Jim Lehrer eventually became the principal choice of both parties to moderate presidential debates.

And we had room to include things we liked, especially books and the arts. The *NewsHour* profiled artists like young violinist Midori and jazz trumpeter Wynton Marsalis long before I heard of them anywhere else.

One of my favorite interviews was with Margaret Mee, an artist who had devoted her life to documenting the rare flowers of the Amazon before they became extinct through development. She was in her eighties, with white hair tied in a black ribbon, and she captivated me as she described and showed film of her last journey into the upper tributaries of the Amazon to paint the rare moonflower. She captivated our audience, too. A few days later, back in England and driving with her husband to Buckingham Palace to be honored by the queen, Margaret Mee was killed. We reran her interview, to even greater response.

Another favorite was a farewell interview with Barry Goldwater in November 1986 when he announced he was retiring from the Senate. Candor drove him to the end.

In his office, his degenerative arthritis now advanced, he sat in a straight chair, leaning on a cane between his knees. He talked about 1964 and the lasting effects on the conservative movement. When one tape roll had been used, I thanked him, pleased that I had such a warm reminiscence. As I stood up, Goldwater said, "Well, aren't you going to ask me about the Iran arms sales?"

It had just come out that the Reagan administration had been selling arms to Iran.

"If I turned on the camera, what would you say?"

"I'd say it was the goddamned stupidest foreign policy blunder this country ever made."

"Turn on the camera."

And when I asked the question, Goldwater obliged in words pretty nearly as salty, ". . . a dreadful mistake—probably one of the major mistakes the United States has ever made in foreign policy."

It so happened that Jim Lehrer was having lunch with President Reagan that day with a few other journalists. Before he went, I told Jim what Goldwater had said, and during lunch he told Reagan. The president went white, began conferring with aides, and a few hours later the White House started mounting the explanations that distanced the president from what grew into the Iran-Contra scandal and threatened his presidency. We led the program that night with Goldwater's comments.

. . .

In 1988, I was in Moscow for the moment I thought effectively ended the Cold War. At the climax of a summit meeting, Ronald Reagan and Mikhail Gorbachev strolled out of the Kremlin into Red Square. There, in a crowd of media and security people, Reagan put his arm around Gorbachev. It was another year before the Berlin Wall came down, but Reagan's gesture told the story.

Reagan was a constant puzzle. He appeared—and private accounts confirmed—uncannily absent, detached, out of it. Yet he repeatedly demonstrated a gift for the gesture, timing, and voice that caught the hearts of Americans. In addition to his own instincts, his career in Hollywood must have been a superb education in what grabbed his countrymen. In politics he could effortlessly apply the myths and archetypes that Hollywood had polished for generations.

And what was more American than that? Or more disconcerting to his vice president and successor, George Bush the elder? Here was an American leader of wide experience and knowledge, but as tone-deaf and gesture-impaired as Reagan was sure. It was painful to watch Bush trying to force his patrician instincts into a populist mold—pretending he liked pork rinds but ignorant of bar code scanners at the supermarket checkout.

Covering many of these leaders over the years, noting the different American traits they personified, I was absorbing lessons about the country. When I was particularly upset with a president, I gradually learned not to make him, as many foreigners do, the Great Satan. Foreigners, immigrants, have to learn what everyone who grows up here knows instinctively: any president, any majority in Congress or the Supreme Court, is not the whole country. You can revere them or despise them and work to replace them, but they are not the whole ball of wax. They are temporary phenomena. They may do marvelous things, they may screw things up for a while, tilt toward this or that interest, make foreigners tremble in their beds, but they pass on and the country's true values endure. That knowledge brought my sensible friends through times and policies they hated. As I learned to think that way, I became comfortable with America.

. . .

As the 1980s advanced and the *NewsHour* settled into its form, I was able to do many other projects: hosting *Live from Lincoln Center*; interviewing Arthur Rubinstein for *Great Performances*; playing the Alistair Cooke role in series like *Edward and Mrs. Simpson* and *Edward the King* for a network assembled by Mobil Oil, and for *Tinker, Tailor, Soldier, Spy* on PBS. For Global Television in Toronto, I interviewed people for a series of celebrity interviews, the most interesting being Muhammad Ali.

One thing struck me every time I met another seemingly larger-than-life American: there is a quality here that lets personality blossom to its fullest, even wildest expression. In horticulture, it is true, many parts of the U.S. lie in agricultural zones where favorable conditions make everything grow more luxuriantly than farther north. So, something in the cultural soil fertilizes American personality, cultivating extravagance; a garden of good and evil in which all species grow with abandon.

That certainly fit Muhammad Ali, in whose life so many strands of recent American experience came together—racism, bigotry, black pride, the appeal of Islam, Vietnam War conflicts, the worship of great athletes, even wit and humor. Whether hated for his arrogance or loved for his genius in the ring, Ali could justly claim to be "The Greatest of All Time." He was the first boxer to win the heavyweight title three times and he revolutionized the sport. He had been, shamefully, stripped of the title for refusing to serve in Vietnam, then after three inactive years had won it back.

I interviewed Ali when he was thirty-six, shortly before he lost the title to Leon Spinks, only to come back to win it for the third time. We met in his home, a French château reproduced in Chicago, surrounded by an iron fence, the grass uncut, a Rolls-Royce in need of washing at the door. Buses of tourists kept driving by. Ali asked us to remove our shoes because his wife was particular about her thick white carpets.

It was the morning after an exhibition bout that had left him moving indolently. While the camera crew set up, Ali lolled on the grand center staircase of the mansion, sprawled over half a dozen steps, chatting with us, yawning, stretching. His wife, very pregnant, was just upstairs, perhaps within earshot, but Ali began boasting of women he'd had, implying just recently, and how successful he was in that. It was strange that this man, who awed the masculine world with the power that symbolized masculinity in our culture, needed to preen himself thus, to strut his virility in this crude way. It was as though a different personality were temporarily in residence. I wasn't sure he was telling the truth.

His physical presence was impressive, like some beautiful specimen in a zoo; his body still perfect, moving with a slow fluidity. Yet you knew he was capable of lightning speed in the ring. He made me think of a jungle cat at rest, a panther it would be pleasurable, if foolhardy, to stroke.

In the interview he gave us what we wanted, the familiar tale of his life. At one moment I quoted some critical remark about him. He leaped up and grabbed me by the throat, mugging for the camera, pretending to strangle me. To feel those large hands tightening around my neck was one of my more interesting journalistic experiences.

The extra income from these ventures let me fulfill a lifelong ambition and buy a sailboat, which I named *Moonlighter* and began cruising in New England waters. Two more boats followed—any sailor knows the escalating ambition—and the cruising range widened. That brought me into another part of America that spoke particularly to me, the coastline of Maine. It is not as pristine as the coast of Nova Scotia, but its many sheltered bays and islands make the waters east of Portland sublime for cruising sailors.

On one trip we were anchored in a quiet bay, almost like a pond, sheltering from a storm outside. A lobsterman motored in to empty his pots. I rowed the dinghy over to ask if I could buy two lobsters. Yes, he said, $2.25 each. He gave me the lobsters and

I gave him a $5 bill. As it was raining hard and he was heavily mobled up in foul weather gear, I said, "That's fine like that."

"No," he said, and he proceeded to lift up, unzip, and unbutton three layers of clothing and dig out two quarters to make the right change. Another scrap of American character, but most typical of Maine. The lobsters tasted all the better for it.

Then sailing was curtailed for several summers because I spent all possible weekends and time off the *NewsHour* working on *The Story of English*.

The sheer fun of exploring the language—always a fascination of mine—was enhanced by the pleasure of the company, the English writer Robert McCrum, whose idea it was, and the producer Bill Cran. We traced English from its earliest origins and how differently it had evolved in becoming a global language; how MacNeils, coming from the same Scottish stock, would speak differently in New Zealand, Australia, North Carolina, or Nova Scotia. The most electrifying moment for me came in a sequence tracing the way settlers from different parts of the British Isles had determined American regional speech patterns to this day by where they landed in America, the earliest in the generation after Shakespeare's death. We had John Barton, one of the founders of the Royal Shakespeare Company, recite the opening lines from *King Henry V* in the accent he thought Shakespeare might have used, the Gloucestershire/Warwickshire dialect of broad vowels and hard "r's". A little later we cut to a preacher on Tangier Island in Chesapeake Bay and the resemblance sent a shiver up my spine.

The series took three years to complete and made us very proud. The book and tape series became a standard reference work, but also worked as entertainment, pulling large audiences.

. . .

Lehrer and I not only became closer friends as we worked together but business partners. In the late '70s we were both getting job offers from commercial networks, with the implied promise of riches, but neither of us wanted to give up the independence our program offered.

Jim Griffin, an agent with the William Morris Agency, suggested that we make a partnership, saying we were more valuable as a team than separately. So we formed MacNeil-Lehrer Productions, which became producer of the *NewsHour* and other programs, including *The Story of English*. Soon others wanted to join us, the most interesting early approach coming from Al Neuharth, founder of *USA Today* and head of the Gannett company. For five years we became MacNeil-Lehrer-Gannett Productions, until they decided we were not going to be a profit center. But our partnership had given Jim and me enough of an ownership stake in our own work to satisfy us and let us ignore other approaches from the networks. That stake was deepened in 1995 when Liberty Media bought a two-thirds' interest in MLP.

These ventures rooted me even more deeply in New York City, as did my personal life. In 1984, Jane and I were divorced and I married Donna Richards. Nothing in life is as tidy as that sounds, and it wasn't. Donna and her husband, Joe, had become our friends. Donna was a keen sailor and Jane wasn't, nor Joe. Jane kept urging me to take Donna on trips with other friends, which happened, quite innocently, for two years. When Jane said once, "You're going to fall in love with Donna, she's just your type," I protested, honestly, that it wasn't so. But . . . eventually it grew obvious that Donna and I were compatible in many ways Jane and I had long recognized we were not. When we admitted that, it was hell for a while for everyone, but especially for Alison and Will, aged fourteen and eleven, who were hurt and angry because we had kept our ruptures better hidden than we knew. It took years to earn their trust back.

· · ·

The more I felt at home in the U.S., the more my citizenship, a subject dormant from the NBC days, resurfaced. Many things prompted me. In 1990 the Radio Television News Directors Association gave me their annual award and made a point of saying I was the first recipient who was not an American.

Coincidentally at this time, I learned a lot more about my roots in the U.S. Besides the name Breckenridge from my southern grandmother, I had been given a second middle name, Ware, from my father's side of the family in Massachusetts, where a Robert Ware from England was granted land in 1642. Two of his descendants fought in the Revolution. A Joseph Ware lost an arm at the Battle of White Plains and his brother, John, fought at the siege of Boston and the Battle of Bunker Hill. A third brother, Henry, became a Unitarian minister and a professor of divinity at Harvard. One of his sons, yet another John Ware, was a professor of medicine at Harvard and his daughter, Frances, brought the McNeils into the picture.

From photographs and a diary she left, Fanny Ware was a striking, high-spirited young woman with a passion for the theater, especially for John Wilkes or Edwin Booth, matinee idols of the time.

Fanny's older brother Robert, a Harvard-trained physician, was serving in the Civil War; while treating Confederate prisoners in North Carolina, he died from typhoid pneumonia.

Fanny moved to Lancaster, Massachusetts, where her love of theater led her into the arms of William Hurst McNeil. He was a roguishly good-looking fellow, in fact, he resembled the young John Wilkes Booth.

William had been born on the British island of Guernsey in 1837, the son of Neil McNeil, a sergeant in the British army. When he died, his widow took William and two sisters back to her family in Canada. William stayed until sixteen, when he moved to the U.S. and worked in a "pianoforte manufactory," according to the *Boston Herald* years later, when he became notorious.

At twenty-one he was an assistant teacher in a high school in Lancaster. Playbills from 1864 onward show that he often performed on the stage and there presumably caught the eye of the stagestruck Fanny. They were married in 1868 and William rose swiftly from schoolteacher, to assistant cashier at the Lancaster National Bank to cashier in 1874 and eventually president in 1882, with Fanny as one of the directors. The McNeils became pillars of the community, active on boards and committees and in the Swedenborgian Church. They summered in Hyannis.

As a banker, William lent easily and was a daring investor. Someone later told the *Boston Herald*, "He had a perfect mania for speculation which began before he was twenty years of age." His investments included Hyannis real estate, a marble quarry in Rutland, Vermont, and a cattle ranch in Wyoming. He was popular in Lancaster where the *Herald* said people spoke of him "as bluff, good natured and generous, with a great deal of bluster, with no head for business."

Then, on December 30, 1885, late at night, he and the young secretary of the bank, Charles H. Veo, drove in a hired carriage to the nearby town of Clinton, where the bank was located. They rifled the bank of cash and securities worth about $185,000. Then they were driven to Fitchburg and took a train north. At Rutland, Veo got off to hide two carpetbags carrying much of the loot while McNeil continued on to the North.

There was a tremendous hue and cry. Veo was arrested and the carpetbags recovered. The story filled New England newspapers for weeks, with speculation that "Mac" the fugitive had been killed or committed suicide. Eventually it came out that he had gone to Canada.

Fanny, described as "prostrated with shock," endured the scandal in Lancaster for a year and a half, then collected herself, sold their two houses, packed all their furniture, and went north to Canada to join her husband.

Outside the town of North Hatley, Quebec, she bought a farm. There, on a high hill looking south over Lake Massawippi, McNeil could almost see across the U.S. border but, as one paper put it, he was safe "under the petticoats of Queen Victoria," there being no extradition treaty. A year later a reporter friend from Massachusetts found McNeil and asked why he had done it.

William said he had speculated too heavily, particularly in electrical stocks and the marble quarry, speculated with money entrusted to his bank. Bank regulators were getting suspicious and, faced with a collapse of his house of cards, unable to borrow money in Boston, he fled. According to testimony in later proceedings, if he had been patient one more hour in Boston on the day he later robbed the bank, he would have secured the loan he needed. Many businessmen have skated on ice that thin and prospered. Perhaps "having no head for business" in his case meant a lack of nerve to brazen out borrowings he intended to be temporary. Or perhaps he was a century ahead of his time.

When the receivers sorted it out, his marble and cattle investments proved to be sound and valuable. From these and the securities recovered in the carpetbags, all depositors got their money back, but shareholders and owners of trust funds did not, and some were thrown into great distress. The exact amount he got away with remains a mystery.

Eventually, William and Fanny built a larger house in North Hatley and became pillars of that community, active in the Anglican Church and the library committee.

When William died in 1900, the Massachusetts obituaries were surprisingly kind. His death, to the *Clinton Daily Item*, "revives memories both pleasant and sorrowful. Pleasant—to those who remember his genial ways and his deep interest in matters political, social and literary, which to a certain date won him the esteem of the community—to others whose confidence and money he won, and who suffered or will suffer by his acts to the end of their lives."

The paper added: "His wife and children, who were held in high esteem in Canada, were ever welcome guests among Massachusetts friends." Fanny lived among her children and grandchildren until 1912.

The strange thing is that I and my brothers, Hugh and Michael, knew nothing about this until 1990, when Hugh and his wife, Alison, were driving back to Nova Scotia and stopped out of curiosity in the town of Lancaster. When they visited the local library they were handed a stack of newspaper stories about the well-remembered scandal. When we visited North Hatley, we found that the story was widely known there, even mentioned in a local history.

We presume our father knew. My brothers remembered seeing him burn some papers in the early 1950s, when he learned that his own father, Robert Ware MacNeil, who was William's son, had died.

Robert had been sixteen at the time his father absconded. Judging by his letters, he spent much of the next ten years working at Table Mountain Ranch in Calaveras County, California. He refers to the ranch owner as Uncle Jack, so perhaps he was a working guest.

When he finally came back east, he tried a series of small business ventures, all of which failed. He had even less head for business than his father. At thirty-five he married Emily Suzanne Auburn, a dark-eyed, dark-haired girl of twenty-one whose mother ran a boardinghouse in Montreal for traveling theater people. It was she who began spelling the name MacNeil. Their first child was my father.

When Canada entered World War I in August 1914, Robert Ware McNeil impulsively joined the cavalry at the age of forty-five and was shipped overseas. Despite his horsemanship, his mount fell on him during training in England, crushing one leg. The injury so disabled him that he could not go into action in France but was sent home to Montreal. Eventually he retired to Long Beach, California, to live for nearly thirty more years.

So, I was born Canadian in part because my great-grandfather robbed his own bank. More inspiringly, I now knew that at least four of my American ancestors had fought in the Revolution, and I began to wonder what I would have done in 1776. Would I have turned my back on the Declaration of Independence, the most thrilling document in modern history? There is no divine right of kings; the divine right is in the people. It would certainly have depended on my age and circumstances, but if I had been the person I am, with my political reflexes, I can't imagine that I would have been a Tory, a Loyalist, and fled to Canada, to dedicate myself to a willful and autocratic sovereign, advised by a Parliament elected on a corrupt suffrage.

11

THE ANGLO-CANADIAN-AMERICAN

*W*henever it passed through my mind that I should do something about my citizenship, a mist of resistance rose to obscure the logic that having been in the United States the better part of my life, I should claim its citizenship. Occasionally a feeling of alienation could still grip me.

On March 23, 1991, for example, I attended the annual Gridiron dinner, the hot ticket on Washington's springtime circuit of media self-celebration. The Gridiron is a club for print journalists, and television newspersons are sparsely invited. Television may be creeping over print like a flesh-eating disease, but here print holds sway as it did in the presidency of Benjamin Harrison, when these dinners began. George Bush (the elder) was the eighteenth president to attend, to suffer himself and his administration to be lampooned in musical skits.

So much Washington power was represented that night in the outsize Capital Hilton ballroom, three blocks from the White House, that one smart bomb, like those the U.S. had been raining on Saddam Hussein, would have wiped out not only the president and vice president but most of the cabinet, joint chiefs, congressional leaders, several Supreme Court justices, and assorted governors and diplomats, not to mention several hundred journalists splendid in white tie or long dresses.

The dinner takes about six hours and its rituals unrolled that evening according to tradition. The number one Marine Band marched in, its music thrillingly loud indoors. It included, as always, *The Washington Post March*, John Philip Sousa's nod to the press, and all the service anthems or hymns, at which present or former members of each service rose in homage.

Dinner courses were served with long intervals for skits, table hopping, gossiping, and going to the bathroom, where an impressionable fellow might later boast that he peed beside Henry Kissinger.

For President Bush, once derided as a *weenie* or a *wimp*, this evening was an apotheosis, almost elevation into heaven, on the wings of victory from the Gulf War and poll ratings in the '90s. The club president opened the evening by saying, "We meet in a moment of triumph and of gratitude to our valiant armed forces," and never was heard a discouraging word thereafter. Some members of the Bush team were ribbed in the skits, but Norman Schwarzkopf, commander of the Gulf War forces, was eulogized. As for Mr. Bush himself, columnist Mary McGrory later noted, "He heard his wartime *agony* compared to that of Abraham Lincoln." Abraham Lincoln? Gimme a break!

Collectively, these Washington pundits and reporters deemed his popularity so unassailable and reelection so inevitable that they hammered the Democrats unmercifully for not having a candidate suicidal enough to take him on in 1992. Listening to this at the *Washington Post* table was Bill Clinton, governor of Arkansas.

For the finale, the lights went down and a poem was read:

> To each lad, to each lass
> Sent forth with our burden
> On desert and sea to roam . . .
> We sing with just one voice
> Till you're safely home.

Then a solo fiddle played the plaintive tune "Ashokan Farewell" from the Ken Burns TV series on the Civil War, and the words were sung by a tenor and the Gridiron chorus. As they say—and many did—there wasn't a dry eye in the house.

Here were the self-certified press elite having raptures over a war from which their profession had been systematically excluded, venerating the men who excluded them. That had so offended R. W. Apple Jr. of the *New York Times* that he declined to attend the dinner at which he himself was admitted as a Gridiron member. Moreover, they were weeping over the "boys and girls" who had fought perhaps America's least costly war of the century, in which massive force and technology had squashed the Iraqis like cockroaches, although missing the cockroach in chief.

This performance seemed to me so mawkish, that while others mopped their eyes, I tried to rationalize what was going on. Twenty-five years earlier I had felt like weeping over U.S. soldiers being killed, about a hundred a week, in Vietnam; not volunteers, not a professional army, but draftees thrown into a war their government could not convincingly explain.

Now, in 1991, was the journalism establishment exorcising

generational guilt over Vietnam, as part of the excused class who did not fight? Did some journalists accept the guilt the Pentagon imputed to the media for turning America against the war?

I was sitting at the *New York Times* table and beside me was A. M. Rosenthal, the recent executive editor. Rosenthal was also born in Canada but came to the U.S. as a child and was later naturalized. He had told me how moving that moment was for him, to stand up there, take the oath, and make that choice.

I told Abe, "Things like this make me feel I'm not American." It was too much celebration of patriotism, too much sentimentalism. He said yes, but the British and French did the same in World War II. I said that was understandable when fighting for the very survival of your country, but that was scarcely the threat from Iraq.

After the Gulf War, many were referring to "a nation of heroes" and that bothered me. Don't real heroes wait for others to call them heroes? Not today: in the PR presidency, reality may lie in the naming, not the meaning. But then Canadians have trouble with heroes, loathe to make them, and I must have carried a little of that infection too with me.

Waking up the morning after the Gridiron, I decided what I found distasteful was that there had been no sense of proportionality. But when emotions run out of proportion to the apparent cause, our Freudianized age knows what to think.

The experience fed into my internal debate.

.   .   .

Because I was now more politically literate, I could better understand the caring society Canada was creating and found it an attractive, if marginal, contrast with the individualistic, more Darwinian political culture in the U.S.

Canadians have always accepted a larger social role for government than Americans. Though slower than Roosevelt New Dealers to palliate the social wounds of the Depression, after World War II Canadian governments began creating a web of services more like those in Western Europe. Chief among these is a national health system that covers everyone. It is administered by the ten provinces with subsidies, or transfer payments, from Ottawa. No one is uninsured. A person needing treatment for a cut finger or heart bypass surgery presents his Medicare card and pays nothing.

There are failures, especially the long waiting times for access to specialists, or quality-of-life operations, like hip replacements. But I have always defended it, as I do the British system, because I admire the fundamentally humane intentions.

Three of my four children were born under the British service and it saved the life of one of them. William was born in London in October 1970. On Christmas Eve my wife, Jane, took her mother, who had the flu, to our then family doctor in Maidenhead, Berkshire. Will, two and a half months old, went along for the ride. While treating my mother-in-law, the doctor glanced at the baby and said, "That child needs to be in hospital, immediately." They called an ambulance and rushed him to a children's hospital at Ascot. We spent that night and Christmas Day hovering over his oxygen tent, not certain he would live. We had thought the baby had a slight cold. The doctor recognized tracheal bronchitis. Untreated, Will might have died the next time he was put down to sleep. The doctor was not a specialist and like most GPs he was probably overloaded, but he was alert.

Of course the British, like Canadians, pay higher taxes for these and other social services. How high the taxes should be is a never-ending debate. Both systems seem chronically overloaded and underfunded. Politicians seldom fund them adequately, for that would mean taking the heat for even higher taxes. In Canada that means heat from business, which argues that higher taxation makes Canada uncompetitive and causes talent to migrate south. Yet the polls consistently show that large majorities of Canadians want a system that they feel defines their country as a caring society.

It remains an open question—perhaps the biggest question facing Canada—whether further economic integration with the U.S. will force a dilution of social programs.

If a basic platform for health care delivery, leaving no one out, defines Canadians, it defines me too, even though in the U.S. I am one of the majority who have enjoyed generous health insurance as a benefit of employment. I also recognize that the American system, whatever its inequality, has driven a great deal of medical research and innovation.

Canada usually ranks slightly higher than the United States on the quality of life and Human Development Index compiled annually by the United Nations. In 1999, Canada was third in the world, the U.S. sixth. For example, life expectancy at birth was 78.7 years in Canada to 76.8 in the U.S. Canadian society shows similar marginal advantages in such indices as immunization of infants, adult literacy, the percentage of the population living in poverty, and the gap between rich and poor. The figures favor the U.S. with lower long-term unemployment and higher per capita income levels.

One intriguing fact of Canadian life is the low rate of violent crime, in particular homicide. In the year 2000 there were 15,517 murders in the U.S. and 542 in Canada. Adjusting for the difference in population (multiplying by nine) brings the Canadian figure to 4,878—one-third the American rate.

The prevalence of guns in the U.S. may be one explanation. Canada is adamant about gun control. Apart from that, Canadian society is less violent. While it soaks up American movies and television, where violence is often the cathartic solution, and while hockey, Canada's national sport, involves considerable violence, Canadians on the whole do not lash out lethally to the degree Americans do.

And Canada has no death penalty. The last execution was in 1962 and Parliament abolished capital punishment in 1976.

· · ·

Despite such convictions, the logic of belonging in the U.S. grew stronger. The question would come to me at JFK Airport, waiting for U.S. Immigration to let me reenter the country where I earned my living, had my home, professional recognition, yet where I persisted in remaining an alien.

The airport or airline employees, bossy young women in blue blazers, carrying walkie-talkies, would herd us imperiously into lines, talking extra loudly as though we were deaf as well as foreign.

"U.S. passports straight ahead, all other passports in these lines." Sometimes they let permanent residents like me go through the U.S. citizen lines; sometimes they don't. It seems inconsistent, arbitrary. Tonight, no. Our line is too long, doubling back on itself many times. I am irritated hot, late, tired, impatient. I sense from their appearance that many others in the interminable line are, like me, green card holders. We live here, pay taxes here. We have established professional positions here. Some may be frequent business travelers, bringing in talent and investments, others well-to-do tourists impatient to spend their money. There are immigrants with large families presenting their landing papers. There are Danish students, Dominican maids, and Jamaican nurses-to-be, all in the line being pushed around by the woman with the walkie-talkie and the training to say one thing: "U.S. passports through there, the rest here."

She is a U.S. citizen and the rest of us are not. And Donna, the American who can tuck me under her wing on such occasions, isn't here. The aristocracy of being a citizen. Why am I not one? What is it that keeps me in this perverse clinging? What is this silver cord that I won't sever? I hate the exclusion. Is it my self-importance or the prickly heat of nationalism that makes me feel too hot, shrug off my raincoat, and put it on my arm as I push my heavy briefcase with my foot, one space forward.

The line jams up more tightly. It gets hotter. I think, As usual I have chosen the wrong line. The inspector is new. Probably nervous. He takes a very long time with each person. He must have been disciplined for a mistake and is now overcompensating. If I were an American I would breeze through. So why not be an American, eh?

. . .

I had had so many bonding experiences with the American people—moments of trauma like the JFK assassination; I had wept with Americans and for them; I had been present at events that gave me a shiver of comprehension, like Martin Luther King at the Lincoln Memorial, like the New York funeral of Allison Krause killed at Kent State; dozens of such experiences.

President and Mrs. Carter once invited us to a small dinner at the White House. Jane was in Europe and I went with Jim and Kate Lehrer. There were two other couples in the small dining room upstairs. After dinner, Rosalyn took us on a tour of the family quarters. In the Lincoln bedroom she pointed with a smile to where Nixon had Henry Kissinger kneel beside him and pray. In two presidential bedrooms she showed us where, on the edge of the mantelpieces, Jacqueline Kennedy had had inscribed in the white marble, "President and Mrs. John F. Kennedy slept in this bedroom," with the dates of their time in the White House. The same, poignantly, in two different rooms, Mrs. Carter observed.

Then Jimmy Carter led us up a small staircase till we came out on the roof and there, just above us, the Stars and Stripes was fluttering, lit by floodlights. I caught my breath: the effect was so unexpected, moving in a way I couldn't explain, invoking something like affection and pride. Pride? Why was I feeling that? Probably it was the sudden juxtaposition of the intimacy on the domestic scale we had just been enjoying, the unpretentious hospitality of this deliberately citizen-president, with the symbol of America's imperial power floating gently over sleeping Washington. It was like one of those moments in the theater that you feel like a blow, a *coup de théâtre*.

Remembering that evening, it occurred to me that I had invested a lot more of myself in the U.S. than in Canada. In the sense of emotional investment, I belonged to Americans more than to Canadians.

Then there was the matter of the American investment in me,

their faith in my talents, the scope they had given me, the security, the recognition, the friendships, the love.

.   .   .

Nova Scotia made a difference, and the death of my mother. In the summer of 1989 we found the place we had been looking for on the South Shore. We had just seen the advertisement that led us there when my brother Hugh called to say that our mother, Peggy, had died suddenly. Donna and I went to Halifax for the funeral; sure she would have approved, we also went to see the place and decided to buy it.

Owning a piece of my native land has brought me to understand the nature of my ties. With something as tangible as land, the need to cling to the abstraction is diminished. It has served both to end my exile and cement it. Since buying that place, I have spent more time in Canada than in all the decades since I left. It has also given me a stronger sense of identity. I can say more assertively now than in the past, I come from Nova Scotia. That has a faintly exotic ring to Americans, which amuses me. I like the little historical irony of King's College in Halifax and Columbia University in New York both giving me honorary degrees. King's was the original Columbia, with a charter from George II, but it decamped to Nova Scotia during the Revolution. I wore the King's College tie to the Columbia commencement for the pleasure of the historical associations. People at Columbia to whom I explained it just about managed to stifle a yawn. It came to me one day that, given the relative amounts of time I spent in the U.S. and Canada, the odds were that I would die in the States. I was in my mid-sixties and forced to think about wills, and where we were going to live permanently when I retired from the *NewsHour*.

Walking home one fine evening past Lincoln Center, I had the sudden realization: I am a New Yorker! I will always be Canadian in that part of me created by a Canadian sensibility. But that is not all of me. Everything else was grafted onto the Canadian root. I am not a Canadian of this time. Canada still provides some of the flavor of my personality but that flavor comes from another time. I am a Canadian of my generation on whom layers of other experience have been fused. My Canada no longer exists as I knew it. The Canada that replaced it is far more interesting but it has grown up in my absence, and it has outgrown me.

When I added up all the ties that bound me here, memberships, associations, boards, affiliations, friendships, commitments, it was obvious I had nothing comparable anywhere else.

Since 1993, I have been chairman of the MacDowell Colony, America's oldest and largest colony for artists, founded in Peterborough, New Hampshire, in 1907. Every year we give fellowships to more than two hundred promising artists from all disciplines from all over the world, and they think it is a magical institution. Recently a Japanese woman artist worked there. Afterward she told us that she had lived for twenty years in the U.S., had married an American, but had never wanted to change her citizenship. Now she wanted to be a citizen of a country where a place like MacDowell could exist. I feel that way.

We discard a skin microscopically, a cell at a time, growing new cells with infinite patience cell by cell until one day all the cells have changed, you have put on a new skin—and the psychological reality hits you.

It is less a decision than a process, a psychological journey, highly emotional at moments, until at last one day you realize the journey is over. You have arrived. You have gone farther than you knew. Your psyche has moved beyond your conscious awareness.

. . .

I applied for naturalization with an immigration lawyer's help, filling out the paperwork, finding proofs of marriage and divorce, and income tax returns for the past five years. I got fingerprinted and applied for an interview date. Months later the INS picked a date when I was committed to be in Jackson, Mississippi. So the lawyer sent them a letter explaining, requesting an alternative date.

The Jackson commitment was to speak at Millsaps College and spend the next day with the writer Eudora Welty.

If America designated its great artists as national treasures, as Japan does, Eudora would surely be one. When I add up what appeals to me in American character, Eudora was one of the brightest gems. She had taken a shine to Jim and me from watching the program, as she had to Roger Mudd and Charles Kurault. Several years earlier she had asked me to speak when her book of photographs from the '30s was launched.

Donna and I had brought her a bottle of Maker's Mark, her favorite bourbon, and she insisted we open it then, at ten in the morning, and have a drink. Physically frail at eighty-seven she was sparkling and slyly witty as always in conversation, speaking in that intimate Mississippi voice you can hear in her own taped reading of stories like *The Optimist's Daughter*. She told us stories all that morning and over dinner that evening.

In the early '30s she attended Columbia University and lived in the women's residence. The woman in charge regularly gave out free concert and theater tickets to the students. When Eudora asked why she never received any, the woman said she'd assumed from her accent that she wouldn't be interested in such cultural activities.

Eudora told us about being invited to visit William Faulkner. Very impressed, she dressed carefully and drove from Jackson to Oxford, where Faulkner suggested they go sailing. To reach his boat she had to wade through mud in her good shoes and stockings. They sailed around the lake for several hours. Faulkner didn't say a word, and she was too intimidated to talk to him. When they reached the shore, she waded back through the mud, thanked him, and drove back to Jackson.

. . .

Months went by and I didn't hear from INS. When my lawyer pressed them, they said they had closed my file when I did not appear for the first interview. They had either lost his letter, and a followup, or ignored them. Eventually they gave me another date, a year after the first. At the interview I correctly answered the ten questions like, Who are the two senators from New York State? But when I gave the woman my passport she said, "This is only two years old. We need it for five years." I said that was my current passport, two years old. No one had mentioned anything more; besides, in the required paperwork I had submitted a list of all my trips out of the U.S. since 1971, the date of my last green card.

"No matter. We need a passport record for five years." Then she told me my fingerprints were out of date. They must be taken no longer than fifteen months before the interview. I said they would have been if the INS had not caused the delay by closing my file.

Already keyed up emotionally at this big step, I went outside to see Donna and the lawyer. I was ready to tell INS to stuff it. What did they think I had done, altered my fingerprints? But the lawyer calmed me down and took me across the street to be fingerprinted afresh. Then I went home to dig up the old passport.

More than two years after my application, I learned in early 1997 that I had been approved and would be sworn in on a day in April.

That morning Donna and I joined a long line of about-to-be citizens outside the auditorium at Police Plaza in lower Manhattan. Inside this huge utilitarian space there was a long wait, with sappy music from a radio station piped in. When the auditorium was full, the ceremony began. The local INS director addressed us, telling us our duty to vote and serve on juries, nothing inspiring, then she led us, right hands raised, through the Oath of Allegiance.

> I hereby declare, on oath, that I absolutely
> and entirely renounce and abjure all allegiance
> and fidelity to any foreign prince, potentate,
> state or sovereignty, of whom or which I have
> heretofore been a subject or citizen; that I
> will support and defend the Constitution and laws
> of the United States of America against all
> enemies, foreign and domestic; that I will bear
> true faith and allegiance to the same; that I will
> bear arms on behalf of the United States when
> required by the law; that I will perform
> noncombatant service in the armed forces of the
> United States when required by the law; that I will
> perform work of national importance under

civilian direction when required by the law; and
that I take this obligation freely without any
mental reservation or purpose of evasion; so
help me God.

Abjuring allegiance to any foreign prince or potentate gave me no qualm. Privately I had abjured Queen Elizabeth and Prince Charles long ago, believing the monarchical connection an anachronism.

Another meaning for *abjure* is to swear perpetual absence from, for example, one's country. Well I certainly wasn't doing that. I knew that when I put my hand down from the oath, I would not only be an American citizen but still Canadian—and through no purpose of evasion on my part.

The Canadian government decided in 1977 that a Canadian who officially renounced his Canadian allegiance to become an American citizen was still a Canadian: Ottawa would ignore the renunciation because it was made under a foreign law. In fact, the year in which I became an American citizen, I was made an officer in the Order of Canada.

Many other countries, including the United States, have now made similar rationalizations. When I got an American passport a few weeks later, it noted the right to dual citizenship.

So now I am a Canadian-American, or what may become increasingly relevant, a North American. Dual citizenship is a step toward a North American citizenship, which most accurately describes what I am. It is also a step toward a less narrowly defined sense of nationality that, given the inexorable drive toward more global interdependence, could be the wave of the future, however disinclined Americans may be at present to see it.

My own children represent that future. Three of them live in London and have British citizenship, which also makes them citizens of the still-growing European Community. Cathy is a dancer, Ian a stage designer, and Will is a film editor, who also has American citizenship. My only purely American child, Alison, is a social worker who lives in Cambridge, Massachusetts, with her husband David McKee and their daughter Neely, my granddaughter. Donna is American but the rest of the family—brothers, sister, nieces, and nephews—are all Canadian. Our family ties mean more than our nationalities.

If there had been no emotional catharsis in becoming an American citizen, I did notice two differences. I felt freer to express my opinions about America and a new tolerance creeping into my attitudes, amusement instead of irritation, for instance, at America the Great Moralizer.

When the scandal over Bill Clinton's sexual relations with Monica Lewinsky obsessed Washington in 1998, the world watched astonished. So did I, but with the new luxury of being an observer not inside the competitive maelstrom every day and I did not react as much of broadcast journalism did.

As usual, *The NewsHour with Jim Lehrer* was a model of restraint and good sense. It was Jim to whom Clinton first lied publicly about Lewinsky and, as many in our office said, You don't lie to Jim Lehrer!

But for the rest of broadcast news, I found myself as disgusted at their behavior as they professed to be at Clinton's.

In a society awash in sex—its industries of advertising, merchandising, modeling, clothing, and cosmetics retailing; magazine covers, movies, TV dramas, and sitcoms—all swimming profitably in a sea of near-porn chic and titillation; a commerce that keeps the society, like an insatiably concupiscent adolescent (advertising's prime target) just on the edge of arousal, we were busily destroying an otherwise talented president for having illicit sex and lying about it. And *lying* about it! The oldest lie there is.

And holding the ring at the center of this amazing circus, piously, moralistically, while wallowing in the prurience, was television news, in free-floating nonstop Monica mania—daily, hourly, minute by minute—happily yapping away, yapping the institutions of democracy into farce.

Amazed at this spectacle, I was delighted that two-thirds of the American people, however embarrassed themselves by Clinton, resolutely opposed this lubricious pursuit by the media, Kenneth Starr, and partisan moralists in Congress.

I was glad I was not working as a journalist because I would have had to surmount a strong personal prejudice. I had spent a few hours with Kenneth Starr after he became special prosecutor, when we were among the judges for a debate at Princeton. It rarely happens that I take an instant, visceral dislike to someone, but I did to Starr.

We were alone for a while and something in his manner provoked me to say, teasingly, "How does it feel to have a president by the balls?" Perhaps I was carrying my new freedom a little far but I didn't care. His reaction—a sudden huffing up, like a male pigeon aroused, ruffling his feathers in coy disavowal of any pleasure in this task, yet protestations belied in a sensuous pursing of his lips—gave me instant intuition that my thrust had hit some mark. When his subsequent behavior appeared to confirm my intuition, a majority of Americans seemed to share it. Yes, I decided, when the people show better sense than the pundits in Washington—this *is* my country.

The Clinton scandal amused the outside world because nothing so satisfies humanity as to see the moralizer discomfited. Seen from abroad, America has a way of wrapping itself not just in the flag, but in the banner of righteousness and the mantle of the Almighty, as though all were exclusively American property.

. . .

September 11 has made us fearsomely aware of how many people around the world are inflamed by an American quality we most prize in ourselves. We are agents of change, the prophets of restlessness and novelty. We merchandise all our innovations, moral and material, and export them to the world. That arouses fundamentalists both out in the world and here at home. America promotes whatever moral relativities suit us at the moment and some moral absolutes (for example, on birth control and abortion) when it suits us in a society in constant flux—very much a work in progress.

The changes in U.S. society just in the forty years I have been part of it have been profound, making the country vastly more tolerant of its own diversity, a better reflection of the world's diversity—racial, ethnic, religious—that America represents.

But has America become a better world citizen? Many think not when they see the U.S. using its unique power to shoulder aside international commitments or treaties it does not like. A sense of exceptionalism encourages boastfulness, arrogance, swaggering, and unilateralism—all the things that irritate even close friends.

America paints its patriotism in bold colors. Inventing itself, the U.S. had to instill a sense of nationhood from scratch, without a king or national religion as its focus. The result was a bristling sense of country, often exhibitionist, and hypersensitive to criticism. In *Democracy in America*, Tocqueville noted that an American tended to take any criticism of his country as an attack on himself.

> The consequence is that his national pride resorts to a thousand artifices and descends to all the petty tricks of personal vanity. Nothing is more embarrassing in the ordinary intercourse of life than this irritable patriotism of the Americans.

That was in the 1830s. Today the United States is older than all but a handful of nations and more powerful than any other, yet, newly vulnerable, it needs the world's good opinion more than ever.

12

SEPTEMBER 11, 2001

We seldom watch television in the morning, finding the breakfast shows too competitively winsome, cable news too yappy and aggressive, preferring to read the *New York Times* in quiet while dipping into Don Imus on the radio. That day I was about to walk to my office eleven blocks away. A day so lovely called for a little detour through Central Park. Almost simultaneously a New York friend and my son Will in London called to say, "Turn on the television!" Thus we saw the second plane hit the World Trade Center.

Stupefied, numb, unbelieving—like millions around the world—we then watched both towers collapse and stayed for hours in front of the television. We went outside, but our street on the Upper West Side is about five miles north of Ground Zero and, staring down Columbus Avenue, all we could see was a distant haze of smoke and dust. I itched to go down there but I had no police credentials; I would be a tourist—in the way. We retreated to the television, impressed with how the local newspeople, so inured to hyping stories, adapted to events that needed no hype. Television all afternoon, all evening, and all the next day, transfixed. We couldn't get a long-distance line, but eventually friends and family outside New York, in Canada and England, got through to ask, Are you all right?

Almost catatonic from two days of television, I called Jim Lehrer to ask if I could help out, and he suggested I do some pieces for the *NewsHour*. It was therapy for the pressing need I felt, like everyone, to do something useful; although I quickly learned how hard it was to remaster the *NewsHour* techniques after six years off the program.

As I began to move around our neighborhood and more widely in the city, I felt like a different person. Walking in New York—one of my favorite pleasures—I usually wore the city's closed look, seeing but appearing not to. Now I noticed I was looking closely at everyone passing, seeing in the faces of New Yorkers eyes equally hungry for reassuring contact, and feeling a warm affection for each touch of that shared humanity.

At every turn was a reason for tears: the photographs and descriptions of missing people posted in large collections and singly everywhere, on lampposts, telephone booths; in all the tiny signs of solidarity among New Yorkers, their pride in being New Yorkers, which I shared. The instant street theater New Yorkers made of their grief, as in Union Square, looking like a peace sit-in from the '60s, guitars, candles, and longhaired girls weeping. In no time mannequins in Fifth Avenue shop windows were dressed patriotically. Commuting SUVs were sprouting the Stars and Stripes.

And Rudy Giuliani, the most bristly and cantankerous of mayors, was reborn—brave, lovable, inspiring.

On West 84th Street we passed a group of schoolgirls about ten years old, one matter-of-factly saying, "If you were lower than the forty-fifth floor, it was okay, but if you were higher, you never made it."

All New Yorkers are used to living with a level of anxiety metabolized into daily life: you don't stand too near the edge as the subway train pulls in, because madmen have pushed people in front of trains. You don't walk across Central Park after dark. It's second nature to keep an eye out, stay alert. But that anxiety level shot up, a collective hypertension: a person in the subway suddenly burst into tears; you saw people start fearfully at a loud noise or at the sound of a plane overhead. At night we awoke at every pass of the patrolling fighter jets, their roar curiously more frightening than reassuring.

Everyone knew someone directly affected. Our window washer's girlfriend worked in the World Trade Center. She got out safely but as she left, someone falling from a higher floor landed near her. Shaken at that terrible sight, she paused and was hit by falling masonry. It tore the flesh off one side of her face and her arm—down to the bone. She was a beautiful woman, he said, proud of keeping in shape. It took a year of agony and surgery before she could return to work and begin to remake her life.

Then, hundreds of personal stories came into our lives in the extraordinary obituaries the *Times* began running, a full page every day, ripping away the anonymity of mass death, making us share the lives of the victims. That increased my desire to look carefully into faces on the streets, in the subway, knowing even more acutely than before that each was living a story as vivid.

In stages, reluctantly, we worked ourselves nearer the site.

After a long illness, Calvin Trillin's wife, Alice, had died the night of September 11, and we went down to Greenwich Village to see him. At 14th Street, police barriers blocked all traffic and we walked half a mile to his house, the air thick with dust and the smell of burning.

We took the subway to city hall and walked around Ground Zero. All buildings from Wall Street to the Hudson were still coated, plastered, with gray dust as thick as blown insulation. The churchyard of Trinity Church was a foot deep in business papers—the same gray color—blown out of imploding buildings. There were growing shrines of pictures, flowers, candles, and then teddy bears, baseball caps, sweatshirts, flags, and posterboard cards with hundreds of messages. Giant trucks rumbled empty down Broadway to return up West Street filled with twisted steel, debris, and human remains.

Ground Zero could not be comprehended from television. You needed the breadth of our human field of vision to grasp how far it stretched—over sixteen acres. You needed the modest stature of a human to be dwarfed and awed by the towering mountain of wreckage. They estimated 1.6 million tons of steel and concrete lay there from the demolished buildings—as though three dozen of the giant ocean liners that used to dock just up the Hudson had crashed in one heap. Except in this heap, the enormous pile-driving thrust of the collapsing towers had driven the debris into a densely impacted mass unlike any ruins anyone had ever contemplated; a mammoth version of the machines that crush automobiles into small cubes. And crushed in there were three thousand bodies.

It was then that we watched President Bush address the joint session of Congress, surprised that this man of such meager gifts as an orator rose so well to the need to reassure and inspire the nation. But it was later, at a news conference, when I heard him say, "I know how good we are," that I knew how much had changed in me. September 11 had apparently pushed me over the edge, removed any emotional reservations about becoming an American that lingered from the arid naturalization ceremony. Four years after I became an American citizen by law, I had become an American in my heart.

When I heard that people were saying, Americans deserved it, or, Now Americans will know what it's like, I was appalled and defensive. No rationalization would fit this moment. Whatever might explain turning planeloads of civilians into fiery bombs, nothing excused it morally. The immediate argument over whether the suicide pilots were brave or cowards was, emotionally, beside the point. (Although the rush to silence Bill Maher and Susan Sontag for raising it showed another American propensity: free speech suffers in moments of high patriotism.) Yes, American policies and alliances might have helped motivate the terrorists. Within a few months the Bush administration was tacitly acknowledging as much by modifying its policies, particularly in the Israel-Palestine crisis.

My instinct was solidarity with those attacked. I could not stop imagining and reimagining—time after time—the last moments of the people on those planes, when all their powers of rationalization and reassurance deserted them—and they knew. For a few harrowing seconds, they knew.

Time to explore the causes later, and vital to do so, but not then, in that first wave of incomprehension and emotional identity I felt with Americans. So did the one hundred thousand Canadians who gathered to mourn on Parliament Hill in Ottawa. So did the Londoners, including the queen, who filled St. Paul's Cathedral. All my strands of nationality and patriotism converged when I saw on television the British in St. Paul's singing *The Star Spangled Banner*, and I was in tears again.

I saw American behavior with a new, affectionate understanding. Even the patriotic displays Canadians consider excessive, perfervid, like the opening of the World Series games—the parade of flags, the giant Stars and Stripes held by West Point cadets, the endless renditions of *God Bless America*—I watched full of sentiment. In that feeling was my identity with New York and the city's amazing reaction, both passionate and cool, an element of modesty, of chastened spirit—and typically sardonic humor, especially directed at government efforts to reassure people.

A hardware store near us displayed gas masks "Direct from Israel, $79.95." Soon they were marked down to $49.95, later $29.95. I said to the owner, "They're not moving so well." "Yeah," he said, "but when that idiot Ashcroft gets up with another alert, the price goes up again!"

Listening to George W. Bush, I did not automatically feel that usual derisive distance. I realized clearly: Yes, I know how good America is, and I knew simultaneously how others wish Americans were not so relentless in saying so. But, for the first time, the derisive emotion was softened, made harmless by the other.

A block and a half from our apartment is a fire station that lost seven men. Like so many others, it became an instant shrine of flowers, plants, cards, and candles. When we passed one afternoon, a brass band of young African-Americans was playing for the firemen. We stopped as they began *The Battle Hymn of the Republic*. In the crowd everyone was weeping, including us, including the firemen in their doorway. The next evening we stopped again and Donna questioned a young fireman about how we could help. When she finished, he hugged her and I stepped forward to shake his hand.

"No," he said, "no handshakes," and embraced me in a long hug.

Deeply moved, I walked home, knowing that I had really embraced America.